AN ACTOR'S DAUGHTER

An
Actor's Daughter

ALINE BERNSTEIN

OHIO UNIVERSITY PRESS
ATHENS

Library of Congress Cataloging-in-Publication Data
Bernstein, Aline, 1881–1955.
    An actor's daughter.

    Reprint. Originally published: New York : Knopf, 1941
    I. Title.
PS 3503.E727A63   1987   813'.52   87–15198

ISBN 0–8214–0870–4 (pbk.)

"Long, long into the night, I lay awake,

trying to think how best to tell my story."

AN ACTOR'S DAUGHTER

One

It was one of those December nights of dazzling starlight that we have in New York, a night so cold that the frost had gone deep into the streets, and made the iron of the horses' shoes ring upon the cobblestones like metal on metal. My Cousin Edgar told me this; and he told me that right after I was born that same night, he himself, a little boy of ten, ran all the way from our house on Thirty-fourth Street to the Madison Square Theatre on Twenty-fourth Street, where Daddy was playing, to tell him that he had a little girl, his first child. Edgar ran through the icy streets without hat or coat, his young feet skimming the ground; and he said the stars and the frost made it light enough to read by, if he had felt like it.

They did not want to let him in at the stage door, a panting breathless youngster with noisy shoes, so he ducked under the doorman's arm. Once inside, he explained his business, and tiptoed quietly to the dressing-room. The curtain was still down but the overture was playing. It was low trembling music, and Edgar said it made everything backstage seem terribly quiet. Daddy was fastening his wig to his forehead with spirit gum, and almost fell off his chair with surprise when he saw Edgar in the looking-glass, coming through the door. But he knew what it was about, only he could not give way to his joy because he had to make his entrance almost immediately. Edgar stayed in the dressing-room until the performance was over, and Daddy brought him home in a cab instead of the street car, by way of celebration. They came into the room where I was bundled in a wash basket, and Edgar told me that Daddy was trembling with excitement. He looked at me for a while, holding both my red new-born hands. "Her eyes are like shoe buttons," was all that he could say. It is the sort of thing people say sometimes, when they are deeply moved, and filled with love and excitement. He told me himself about the shoe buttons, and how he went over to the bed where Mama was watching him and gave her a long thankful kiss.

Two

Daddy came of an odd mixed stock, which may or may not account for his temperament. His father was a German Jew, and his mother the daughter of one of the oldest families in Connecticut. The two elements were quiet enough in themselves, but when they came together in my father they fuzzed up like the two parts of a Seidlitz powder when put together in water. His father came to America from a German city. He had a tiny bit of money, a cultivated mind, a handsome person, and the kind of rich and charming personality that we think of as European, and that was so lacking in the worthy New England young men. Through an advertisement he found a position in a dry-goods store in Hartford. The ladies all liked him, and in spite of his humble position and his race, he was invited out to some of the best houses. He sang and played at their parties and taught them how to waltz; he helped them select the most becoming colours for their dresses, tucked artificial flowers among the ribbons of their bonnets, and showed them how to bring life into their sombre parlours, rearranging the furniture and bringing the gaiety of flowers indoors.

In that lovely Connecticut valley, he fell in love with the white houses and their panelled rooms, the doorways, the glass and china, all of the things built and made during that epidemic of taste that spread through New England in the eighteenth century. And he fell in love with my grandmother. She was lovely; she had in her the dignity and beauty and the spiritual value of the New England he found so wonderful. She was living in the house built by her forefathers in 1693, the most beautiful type of house in the world, to my taste; a white pine house, set in its neat garden among green fields, its barns stretched out in homely ample wings, far bigger than the house itself, elm trees dripping their branches on the sloping roof, the design of it all like a phrase of music. The farm lands were rich, sloping down to the Farmington River, and later, when planted with tobacco, made money for the family.

We all went up there to visit in the spring when I was a child, during the week that the shad ran in the Farmington River. There was a family feast; more than a hundred relatives came together for it, to eat the shad. All the visiting cousins lived with cousins who had houses, crowding the houses so that the walls bulged.

The day of the feast we were given big New England breakfasts in the morning, then nothing else until the great meal in the afternoon at five, served in the lower meadow under the trees. The farm boys made roaring fires of hickory logs at noon, so that there were deep beds of glowing wood coals to broil the shad, which had been caught in the morning. It was dished up on long hollowed planks instead of platters, and instead of butter, yellow cream was put over the fish, cream so thick it had to be put on with a spoon. There were boiled greens and baked potatoes.

The taste of the cream over the charred fish makes my mouth water as I remember it; it all went together with the smell of the fires, the long view over the meadow to the white steeple of the church across the river, and the tender rounded froth of the tops of the elms, like green smoke. We ate until we could barely move, then topped it off with chopped lemon pie, a dish I have never seen anywhere but in that family. It was made of black stoned raisins, lemons chopped fine as sand, flavored with molasses, and it had three crusts, the conventional top and bottom crusts with an extra one put in the middle.

Old Mr. Root drove down from his farm above

Windsor Locks to play the fiddle. He was the only one who was not a family connection, but none of the cousins could play and there had to be music. Uncle Ran said music made his food sit. He fiddled for all occasions in the neighbourhood and there was not a tune in the world he could not play. He was crazy about the stage, and considered himself one of the magic band of theatre to which Daddy belonged. After he put up his horse he made a bee line for the table where Daddy served the drinks.

"What'll it be, Mr. Root?" asked Daddy and he gave the name that peculiar New England intonation, as though it was spelled Ruut.

"Just a little sody water, Joe, it's thirsty work fiddling for so many people to dance, and I tell you what, boy," and his Adam's apple rolled up and down in his throat in his silent jocularity, "how about a dash of gin, for my kidneys?" The dash of gin may or may not have worked on his kidneys, but it was wonderful for the fiddling.

When the meal was over and the trestle tables cleared, pitchers of last year's hard cider were set out, and Daddy gave them a song. His fine barytone rode out on the evening air. Maybe it was not the greatest singing, but his voice had a poignant breathy quality that turned you inside out. He said it was a mean trick

8

of nature to make him a barytone; it was the tenors who always came out on top and had the love scenes with the beautiful sopranos, while the barytone either died of a broken heart or had to team up with the contralto, who was always overripe, old, had a dark moustache, and lived on garlic. He said contraltos were made, not born, for he never met a young one, nor one who weighed less than two hundred pounds. However, in spite of his vocal range, he did mighty well with the ladies in real life.

When the beautiful Ellen promised to marry my grandfather, her family refused their consent. They were horrified at the idea of her marrying a Jew, no matter how handsome, promising, and cultivated, and a Jew at that who had no money, that one invariable accompaniment to the race, like brightness to the sun. So she did a strange thing. She left her father's house and went to live in the house of a rabbi in Hartford. There she helped the rabbi's wife take care of the children, she helped with the sewing and the household tasks in exchange for her keep and her education in the Jewish religion. Life in the two households was not very different; there was the same good living, a little kitchen, richer maybe in the Jew's house; the same kindliness and respect for the individual, the same strong family ties and reverence for the elders that made a kingdom of home. Friday mornings instead of polishing the Paul Revere teapot, she polished the old silver wine cups from Augsburg, and the heavy silver candlesticks to be used for the Friday night dinner, that loveliest of all family rituals. Her family missed her, for they loved her, and they asked her to come home and marry the man she loved. But she stayed in the rabbi's house a full year until she learned all the ritual of the Jewish faith and could cook as well as the rabbi's wife. She was married in his house under the canopy, and the good man said he felt the same joy as though his own daughter was marrying. She was a pious Jewess all her life, far more faithful to the forms than her husband, and she named her first child, my father, Joseph, after her friend and teacher.

While Ellen was learning to be a Jewess, my grandfather, who was a shrewd man under his rather fancy exterior, started to build up a business for himself. He borrowed money from the husband of his sister in New York, rented a small shop in Hartford, and went to Europe on a sailing vessel. He brought back enough foreign goods to stock the shop. He knew what the customers wanted; better still he knew what he could make them want. His stock was dress lengths of silks and gauze and embroidered muslins, shawls and scarves and handkerchiefs, gloves and gold-headed canes, little lace parasols, odds and ends of jewelry, not too valuable, and small antique objects of amber and ivory. It was a varied stock, not too much of anything, and sold like wildfire. Every piece of merchandise in his shop was bought by him because he thought it was fine. They opened the shop the day after their marriage, they wanted no honeymoon; they only wanted to be together and begin life.

My grandmother grew very fat after her children were born, and I have heard that his attentions to the lady customers went beyond the strict line of business. Or that might have been one of the secrets of his success; for the shop prospered, and when the Civil War came he had enough money so that he could afford to equip a regiment of volunteers from Connecticut. He saw active service with them, until he was lightly wounded and honourably discharged. Business was dead in Hartford, so he decided to move to New York. He thought, too, that it would be fine for his children to have the advantages of education and life in the city. He did fairly well, made a living, but he was too soon for New York. A little later, when the wives of skyrocket millionaires were sending Mr. Worth a thousand dollars for a dress, he would have made a fortune.

When Daddy graduated from school, he did not want to go to college, although that was his father's ambition for him. He wanted to get out into life. He did not know what he wanted, he had a boy's vague passion. He sold newspapers morning and afternoon to make pocket money and read every minute of his spare time. He went to the Mercantile Library, where his mother had a membership, and he read from the second-hand bookstalls. He read everything he could come by. He saw French books in the library and taught himself the language; he bought an English Bible and a French Bible, and learned by comparing them sentence by sentence. He knew it was not the kind of French to do him much good, so he started to read the Paris newspapers at the Mercantile Library. He learned the language and he liked what he read. For practice he translated articles and poems into New York English, then did the harder job of translating New York papers into French. He was at heart a poet, and managed in his translations to keep the form and lightness of the French verse, adding a flavour and touch of his own, like the feel of the hand of a good cook in a sauce.

Daddy never told me how he and Mama met, but he told me how he came to be an actor. His favourite bookshop, the one he honoured most with his free trade, was kept by a Scotsman named MacNeill. Mac-Neill lived in a big basement room behind his shop.

It was the habit of his young customers, most of them of about the same financial standing as Daddy, to congregate in the evenings around the fireplace of Mac-Neill's back room and indulge in glasses of tea and a lot of heady conversation. Most of them were glad of the warmth and companionship, all of them were interested in books and writing. They had wonderful hours of talk in that back room, most of them young men knowing for the first time that great human delight, the sharing of ideas and opinions. I have known it, and it is a joy that belongs not only to the young; but the young are full of freshness, discovery, and hope. Among them was a young man a little more prosperous than the rest, a man named Harlan, who had a steady job as poetry editor for a magazine. In those hot evenings beside the fire they showed each other their stuff and Harlan bought one of Daddy's poems for his magazine.

That night, instead of parting outside in the street and going their separate ways, Harlan put his arm through Daddy's and asked if they might walk together part of the way home. It was raining, for Daddy said he remembered the long reflection of the lamps on the wet streets and how something inside of him felt just like those lines of light. The dampness felt good on his face after the heat of the fire, and the rain fell on Harlan's hair, making it curl like a million wire springs.

"We've talked a lot together, Joe, and I must tell you how much I like you, you have mind and talent, a rare combination. But you have more. You have the stuff of an actor."

He stood still in the rain, his eyes blazing.

"I've never told you my real ambition, what is at the core of my mind and heart," and he touched his right hand to his forehead, then rested it on his breast. It was a true histrionic gesture, and his body was tense with excitement.

"I am writing a play!"

The years go by, and young men stand in the rain or the sun or under the stars, and they tell this wonderful thing to their friend, and the theatre lives for ever. They discover it, the young men and women, and it lives for ever. For it is the great platform, where life does not die, but is re-created and lives again, where the finger points, and the heart is moved to tears other than its own.

"I've watched you for months. You have the fire in your eye and one of the finest voices I have ever listened to; when you recite it resounds like an organ. You are handsome enough and powerful enough to affect thousands of people. For they must fall in love with Joe, that is the secret. Cast your spell, then they will listen to you. Kindle them, then pour on the fuel, and, God, what a conflagration we can make!"

Then he told Daddy that he was young, not rounded enough yet for the play he was writing, but he said he would teach Daddy how to learn to act.

"You must look at life with different eyes, you must look both at the surface and deep down into it, you must search the sources. Nothing is too small to study, don't believe that anything or anybody is too insignificant to study—not to an actor or a playwright. Watch them, Joe, watch man, woman, and child, their manners, their walk, how they use their hands and their feet, their eyes and their mouths, and how they breathe through their noses; what they wear and how they wear it. Find out for yourself what makes a joyful face look joyful and what gives the look to a face of agony. Watch and learn, and you will be so rich you can have a whole world for yourself and it will be yours for ever; the stage is the great democracy, where a beggar is equal to a king."

Harlan had the elements of a great teacher; that was a wonderful thing for a boy to hear in the formative time when Daddy heard it. For he was a boy filled with creative desire, with all the gorgeous strands of his life in his hand, ready to weave it into its design; but the design comes through according to the weaver, and

15

with all his gifts some devil saw to it that he was not given stability, sense, and the sterner qualities that were inherent in my mother.

Harlan wrote his play, he wrote it over and over again, and it was enormously successful; he wrote a part into it for Daddy. I have his photograph taken in the part. In the picture he is seated on a prop balustrade, one foot on the ground, the other on the rail, his elbow resting on his knee; he wears low-cut, low-heeled leather shoes, long white cotton stockings, knee breeches, a loose short jacket, and a white shirt open at the neck. His wig is cut round like a Dutch boy's hair, only untidy, the locks ruffled as though a breeze had blown them, and on his head is a wide dark felt hat, turned up in front and showing all of his handsome face. His full eyes, luminous and arresting, look straight into the eyes of the beholder. The effect of the photograph is theatrical. It is like all the actors in the world. Only his special beauty is added to it. It looks like an unfamiliar happy Hamlet, a Hamlet whose mind had really crossed the borderland of reason into blissful ignorance of evil. The audiences fell in love with him, everybody did, and it was the worst thing in the world for him.

In those years he worked with Harlan, he learned an enormous amount of poetry, and most of the principal Shaksperian parts; in fact he knew more of the Shakspere plays than any actor I have ever known. It was part of the task he set himself; and by the time he was playing in stock companies he was able to learn a long part letter perfect in two readings. But his poetic attitude to life was his own, a gift from God. It lifted him from the ordinary actor into something singularly exciting. He taught me poems, accenting all the rhythms, to help me walk to school in the mornings, and "Tiger, Tiger, burning bright," quickened my feet toward school through the dreary morning streets. One day my teacher, Miss Haight, read us "The Tiger" by William Blake. She cleared her throat and read it through, dull and tuneless, but before she finished I jumped up and shouted: "Not William Blake, it is my father's!" But she showed it to me, printed in the book.

He recited to me, all hours of the day, even in the night. "Listen," he said. He came into my room, waking me, well toward morning, for I could see a trace of daylight in the window. "This is better than sleep:

"These our actors,
As I foretold you, were all spirits, and
Are melted into air, thin air;
And, like the baseless fabric of this vision,
The cloud-capped towers, the gorgeous palaces

17

The solemn temples, the great globe itself,
   Yea, all which it inherit, shall dissolve,
And, like this insubstantial pageant faded,
Leave not a rack behind. We are such stuff
      As dreams are made on; and our little life
      Is rounded with a sleep."

Tears were in his eyes, and made them luminous. He was right, it was far better than sleep. Any child could sleep, but what other one had ever been awakened to such reading?

Three

My mother's parentage was as different from Daddy's as she was different from him. There never were two people less alike. She was not beautiful, unless you loved her; when you did, the loveliness of her character shone out like a radiance. It was a soft radiance, and her brown eyes reflected the sadness of her race. She was small, but so well proportioned that you didn't think of her size. Her skin was golden olive, one even tone over her face and body, except for the rich darkening around the sockets of her eyes. Her hair was superb; it was so long that she could sit on it, it had the satiny brown colour of a chestnut shell, and she wore it in a great looped crown on top of her head, like a heavy turban. She had genius for all the details of daily life, sewed and cooked like a professional, and could make a dollar work like two. Out of scraps and short lengths of stuff, bits of ribbon and felt and feathers, given to us by our more prosperous aunts and cousins, she made all of our clothes, as exquisite and imaginative as the finest things from Paris. Above all, she had a great capacity for comforting and devoted love. It was her tragic fate that the two she loved most, Daddy and Nana, were way beyond her help.

Her father also came from Europe to make his fortune in America. He was a Dutchman, a graduate of the University of Leiden, where he taught law for a few years until he felt he could do better with his life. He had one of those brilliant legal minds that are as much of a gift as a fine singing voice, and it did not take him long to learn the language and pass his New York bar examinations. He made an immediate success, and married a Frenchwoman, who died giving birth to the last of his three daughters. That daughter was my Aunt Rachel, the one we called Nana, the one that I adored.

They always lived high in my mother's family; they had horses and carriages and a coloured coachman named George Washington Goldsmith. They had a brown stone mansion on Thirty-fourth Street, with a high stoop and rooms both sides of the front door, and their own stable in the back. My grandfather had a passion for Thirty-fourth Street; he thought it was the finest street in the city, and it was; it was wide and handsome. He bought up every piece of property on that street that came up for sale, and as each of his daughters married he gave her one of the houses he had bought, regardless of the station in life of her husband. So that on that frosty night when young Edgar ran in the starlight, I was born where Macy's now stands, and my mother's house was just about where the underwear department is at present. He later developed passions for other streets in New York, Seventh Avenue and Upper Fifth and Riverside Drive when it was still a wilderness. When he died he left titles to an enormous amount of property, all mortgaged; the equity had sunk into the ground like soft spring rain.

He died before I was born, but Mama told me a lot about him. He was most luxurious, he wore black broadcloth, the finest linen, a black satin stock, and a long gold watch-chain around his neck, clasped in front with a gold hand. They had loads of company, they had wine and whisky and cigars for everybody, but he had his own special cigars in a closet upstairs, too good for anybody in the world, he said, but Henry Goldsmith.

He married a second time, a scrawny woman, good as gold, and he showered her with presents. He gave her a historic pair of earrings, long pear-shaped pearl drops set with diamonds that had been a present from Napoleon to Josephine. He had identical copies of them made for his mistress, who lived just round the corner on Thirty-fifth Street. Mama said she had an idea that the mistress got the originals, but at any rate every present he gave his wife was duplicated for the big honey-haired Mary Gheen. I knew that girl in later years; after the old man died she opened what she called a theatrical boarding-house, but she only boarded the pretty girls that sang and danced and did their turns at Koster and Bial's, later on moving up to Forty-third Street, with the changing city, where she boarded the girls from the shows at the Casino.

It took a long time to find out that there was no money left in the big Goldsmith Estate. Nana had married a young doctor, with flaming red hair and beard, and the most perfect bedside manner in town; Aunt Mamie had married a handsome fellow from the South who just couldn't get along in business; and Mama had settled in with her handsome actor, who had two years' experience in stock companies and the prospect of a long run in a successful play. The houses on Thirty-fourth Street vanished into air, and their occupants all went their ways.

The life of an actor was uncertain; it always will be; the carefree gaiety, late nights, late risings, and late meals, the easy friendships, the long strolling lazy days, all had to be paid for. Salaries were small, and jobs scarce, and a wife and little girl had to be supported. Aunt Mamie's husband couldn't even act, so she rented a big house on Forty-fourth Street and opened a boarding-house. We went to live with her there, and of all the thousand places I have lived, I loved that almost the best.

You never needed to be lonely in that house. When you felt that dreadful thing coming over you, when you felt that no matter what, you just had to be with somebody or touch someone, someone was always there. Morning, noon, and night the Irish girls were having strong black tea in the kitchen, the brown pot was for ever on the back of the stove. They would give me a cup and it made my tender young tongue shrivel and my teeth feel as though they were rubbing silk. They always talked about the boarders and about their own "fellers." It seemed strange to me how resigned they were to being servants until I knew they all came from a land of pigs and rain and bogs, of five-mile walks to school, knitting socks as they walked, too many brothers and sisters, and not enough to eat. In Aunt Mamie's house they had loads to eat and a roof that never leaked, they got up at seven instead of five, and there was money in their pockets to give the priests and send a little bit home. So on the whole they were better off, although I did not know it. I only knew that they had no freedom to run out of doors when they felt like it, that they had the dark smelly inside rooms on the top floor, that they had to be for ever at the other end of a bell, could not bathe in a bathtub but only in the wash tub in the cellar. They would have changed everything at any time for life in a tenement with the feller when he got a job.

We had a large top-floor room all done in massive walnut brought from the parent house. The bed looked like a gloomy, funny, fancy altar, rising tier on tier at the head, above the mattress. I had a cot that folded up and was shoved under the bed in the daytime, but when Daddy was on the road, I slept in the big bed with Mama. When I woke in the night, for I always have, and I love to, I leaned over and touched Mama's cheek, moving my hand back and forth over its surface. Her cheeks were smooth and soft, smooth as satin and soft as Lyons velvet; there should be a word to describe that softness of a woman's cheek. You say "So soft," but it is more than that, it makes you feel the way certain words do. Safe, and home, if home is what you love.

When I woke early in the morning, her eyes were open, and sometimes she was crying. I tried to draw my hand away, for children hate tears that are not their own; she held me tight and kissed me, and maybe I brought her some comfort; for we dozed until it was

24

time to get up. Daddy went away for long road tours, when there was nothing to be had in New York, and usually sent home enough money to pay Aunt Mamie, sometimes not; they worked hard when there were one-night stands, then they drank up a whole week's salary on a Saturday night spree, with female trimmings. Mama was wonderful about it, she said there were more people ruined by economy than by extravagance. Our family were never quite ruined, but if they had been it would never have been through economy.

Nana's husband, Uncle Ben, had begun his successful career. He was a fine physician, and he claimed that it was as easy to feel the pulse and look at the tongues of the rich as it was to do the same for the poor, and far pleasanter. He was troubled with no ideas of the obligations to humanity of his calling, but he devoted himself to the best of his fine ability to his own patients. He was one of those strong ugly men who can be so attractive to women, and I am sure he could have married all the money he wanted, if he had not met Nana and been bewitched.

She married him for a characteristic reason, because she was in love with somebody else and wanted to teach somebody else a lesson. She was exciting and outrageous and she almost ruined him. She had a splendid figure, tall and round, with the grace of a full rigged ship cutting the water. Her eyes were no colour except when they looked green, her nose was thin and had a slight turn to the left, at its tip, which made you think her face a little queer. She had no trace of Mama's wonderful hair, it was just plain hair with copper lights in it when she came near a window or under the chandelier; but she could twist it into a knot at the back of her head, stick a diamond pin through it, and there was Nana. Other women tried that trick, but none of them had Nana's wrist to turn it with, nor the set of her lovely small head on her neck. With her rather plain face she made you think she was beautiful, and when she walked into the room it seemed that the lights burned brighter.

Her clothes were magnificent, but she always had a little too much on or off, in the wrong place. Her bodice was cut too low, and showed the division of her breasts; her train was too long, and her skirt had too many ruffles underneath, and the silk made a big noise when she walked. Mama argued with her, but "They like it," Nana said, and they did.

She smoked, in an all but smokeless age for women, when only tarts and short-haired Russian Nihilists smoked. She wore too many rings, and refused to wear gloves in the evenings, no matter where they were dining, for she used her hands a great deal to point her

talk, and her talk had an interesting, an arresting tim-
ing. There would be a fraction of a second's hesitation,
a quick breathy plunge, then a long quiet flow. She
would shove her dinner partner with her glittering
fingers, and tell him how much easier it was to con-
verse lying down than sitting side by side. You could
think of much more amusing things to say that way,
she said, than with all these people sitting around and
taking the edge off things. Or she would suggest he
come around some evening, bring his wife if he liked,
and she would cook him a pot roast that would melt in
his mouth. When dessert came on, she would haul out
a package of all-tobacco cigarettes, from a pocket in
the draperies of her skirt; evening bags were trifles
then, holding only a small handkerchief, for no one
powdered in public. When she demanded a light it
caused a sensation, which was doubtless what she
wanted. If it did not come soon enough, she reached
out with her diamond-heavy hands for the nearest silver candlestick and lit up from that. Uncle Ben always
heard and saw her, no matter how far down the table
he sat, and that was the seed of the quarrel that started
in the carriage on the way home, and sometimes lasted
for days.

Discipline was unknown to her. She would have
her wish, no matter what it cost her, nor what it cost

those who loved her. Each piece of indulgence under-
mined her morality until her will was gone, and she
crumbled. She was never selfish in the narrow sense,
she would give the dress off her back, and she had a
beautiful and embracing pity for anyone in poverty
or pain; but she was morally blind to what was near,
and all thought of living was in a dreamy present
which she expected to be indefinitely extended.
Sometimes Mama could influence her, but never for
long.

The first summer we lived in Aunt Mamie's top
floor Uncle Ben had a house in Newport, where his rich
patients took their ailments for the summer, and Nana
had me with them for a month. They had a turreted
wooden house, with red and blue glass panes in the
front door and miles of porch, across the road from a
piece of rocky moorland that went down to the sea.
It was my first time by the sea, the first time I knew
the magic of pail and shovel and unlimited sand, the
little creatures of the water in rocky pools, and the
smell of seaweed and tide, and bayberries and wild
roses.

I presume I played with the little swells who lived
near us and used the beach, but I do not remember
any of them; I remember the walk up to the house
from the beach, and stumbling on a rock and falling

on my pail, gashing my chin, and having Uncle Ben
sew it up with three stitches; and how furious I was
that anything I liked so much as that pail and shovel
could make me bleed.

Nana learned to ride horseback, and was out every
morning with her groom, coming home for lunch
with one gentleman or another. The ladies all wore
black or grey habits with black derby hats, but she
had a light tan habit with a brown derby, and a moss-
green veil that came down as far as her nose in front
and streamed out in the breeze behind. It made her
eyes look like emeralds if you could get a chance to
look at them. Her horse was brown, and no matter
how many people came riding up the road together,
you could tell Nana a mile away.

I usually ate lunch with them in the dining-room,
but when some of the gentlemen stayed I had it on
a tray in the kitchen. The waitress felt sorry for me
and as a treat she gave me my drinking water in a
special glass. She said I could call it my own glass,
because nobody else used it. It belonged to a liqueur
set from the sideboard, a stoppered bottle and six little tumblers, of bright aquamarine glass. The colour
made the water taste cool as I looked through the
glass, drinking. One afternoon I came in hot and
thirsty from the beach and saw my glass on a marble-

topped table that stood in the bay window of the dining-room. Nana kept potted plants on that table and the sun slanted through the pinkish leaves of the begonias and the blue glass, all very beautiful. I looked down through the glass—it was half full of water—and I could see the veins of the marble quiver as the water shook when I touched the table.

In a second I thought how wonderful it was that my glass was there, just when I was thirsty and needed it; I drank the water, but this time it was not cool and magic, it was warm and bitter. Half filled, the glass held only a mouthful, and I had swallowed it before I knew it was strange. I heard a strangled noise, a scream, Nana was running across the room, grey with fright, a small bright object gleaming in her hand. She dropped it and caught me up in her arms and ran all through the big house calling: "Ben, Ben, for God's sake, Ben," but Ben was not there. I wish he could have heard Nana's call, it was probably the only time she ever called him straight from her heart, and he missed it.

She was frantic. The servants, scared by her cries, came from the kitchen and the gardens and the stable; she ordered her carriage and sent the riding groom on her fast horse to find Uncle Ben. The cook made a horrid mess of mustard and water, but I was too frightened to swallow. The groom found Uncle Ben, fortunately he was near by, and he saved my life. By the time he came the morphine was beginning to take effect, and I could not keep my eyes open, it was such a delicious drowsiness, and I didn't want to come out of it. He had two other doctors in to help him, they walked me up and down to keep me from sleep, from the sweet sleep that Nana had intended for herself, but for my young body it meant death. They gave me hot baths and cold baths, they hit me and shook me and put ammonia under my nose. The world was made of grey gauze, my mind had an unwieldy thickness, it went forward into consciousness and backward into space, never quite making it, with a horrid rhythm, in and out like a concertina. A voice babbled in my ear, as though it came through flannel: "Don't go, baby—stay here with us, darling— don't die, baby—take hold of me, darling—don't leave, stay—stay—stay—if you die it will kill her, I will kill her, they know what it was, I can't live without her.— It's three lives, if you try, if you want hard enough, you can stay, you'll be my own little girl—please, baby, stay, and save us—I must save you, baby, darling, baby—Ray, O God—baby—baby—stay—"

He must have been holding me in his arms then, his mouth against my ear. Hands were slapping me;

I felt the sound, but it did not hurt. I wanted it to stop. I wanted sleep.

"Circulation keeping up, back as red as a lobster," I heard, then the voice was gone, and there was the sick loss of myself back into space, trying desperately to hear Uncle Ben, to hold him with boneless, nerveless fingers, trying to do what he asked. Down into deep flowing river, I heard the water lapping, I felt it flowing over me, felt agony, and saw a hand pour a steaming stream from a kettle into the water that covered me. I screamed louder and louder, it was so hot I nearly split my head with my screams. I clutched at the air, I clutched two sleeves on arms that were taking me from the water. I felt the grateful cool of a linen sheet, wrapping around me. With great effort I could keep up my eyelids, he was holding me at an open window. At last I was breathing, I could smell the sea and the fragrance of the seashore verdure; my heavy lids stayed up, so I could see the faint line of lightness in the sky against the black line of the sea at the horizon. I felt once more, I tried to speak, to tell Uncle Ben I could stay, I turned my head to rest on his shoulder, but words would not come, I could only hum: "mm, mm, mm!"

It was enough, he no longer babbled, but I shook against his body with his sobs. He kissed me, softly, so that his beard did not hurt my irritated skin, he kissed my hair, my eyes, my cheeks, and called me his blessed little child. The horrible coming and going stopped in my head, exhaustion took its place and held me in the present of the night.

Four

I was glad to be back in the boarding-house, in our top-floor room, and close to Mama's sheltering bed. She came up to Newport to take me home. I knew I would miss the sea and the freedom, but the tin pail and the blue glass had spoiled it for me. The minute I saw Mama's face, I knew there was something I wanted more. I dread to think what her life would have been had I died, for much as she loved me, she loved her sister even more.

Uncle Ben wanted us to take a house and have them live with us, but Mama said no. I think she was frightened for me. He came to see me every day, and often took me with him on his rounds of visits, in his smart shiny black brougham, with its handsome grey horse. There was a little boy named George who sat up on the box beside the coachman. George would jump down almost before the carriage stopped, dash up the steps of the house with incredible speed, ring the front door bell, dash down again and open the carriage door, carry the doctor's bag with him, and wait until the door was opened. He was dressed like the coachman, in a plum-coloured coat, white doeskin breeches, tight to his legs like the skin of an onion, a high black silk hat with a cockade at the side, and shiny black boots with tan leather turnovers. Only his coat was short, like an Eton jacket, while the coachman's was long, like a Prince Albert. They called such a little boy a tiger, and I presume he was serving his apprenticeship to being a coachman. Those afternoons were a bore for me and I do not know why I went, only that Uncle Ben wanted so much to have me with him. Nana used to tease us and say he had a new wife. He gave her a black look, and she smiled that way she had, only half her mouth smiling upward. He kept pulling one of my curls through his fingers, and he told her he would give me a diamond star. He did; a tiny one, about as big as my thumbnail, but he had a flock of five made for her, to wear across the front of her blue satin evening dress, the largest one as big as a teacup.

He was fond of horses, and took Monday afternoon for himself to drive in the park. Nana used to go with him, but gradually it came about that I went instead. He drove a high two-wheeled yellow dogcart with a pair of fast brown horses. George sat on the back seat facing out, like a wooden image, his arms crossed under his chest; he was like part of the equipage, and only moved when we pulled up somewhere to stop. As the winter came on, Uncle Ben had a coat made for me by Nana's habit-maker, a warm red cloth with an extra cape that hooked on under the collar, and he never let me wear it except on our drives, no matter how cold it was. The first time I wore it we stopped at Macgowan's Pass for a hot chocolate, and I felt smart and beautiful, in spite of all the smart ladies that were there. Hot chocolate was not the usual drink in that place, but they managed to get one up for me. I felt gay and strong after we left the restaurant, and Uncle Ben suggested I learn to drive. He sat me in the driver's seat, my feet barely touched the floor, and he put his right arm around me, guiding my hands, that held the reins. We went slow, until we came to the road around the reservoir. "Now then," he said, and took the whip out of its socket, flicking it over the horses' heads. They started off at a great clip, they knew what was required, and my hair and cape flew out in the wind. That was every Monday afternoon for a whole winter; I learned to drive and master horses, and I learned more than that. I learned from undeveloped sources that a female had certain qualities.

During that winter my sister was born. Daddy was home and we had moved downstairs from the top floor to the third. I had a little hall bedroom for myself. Our finances must have been better, Daddy had an engagement in one of the stock companies for the season. Nana and Uncle Ben wanted me to live with them; he had bought a handsome house on Clinton Place. I stayed sometimes on Saturday night, but I hated the smell of medicines that came into the house from his office, and I thought the Monday drives were enough. I began to be a little afraid of him and his check on my liberty. I could not do this or that, nor wear the clothes he bought me when I pleased, only when I went out with him.

The baby was born in the early afternoon, soon after lunch. I knew what was happening, and I sat at the head of the stairs outside Mama's room so I would miss nothing. I had an inseparable companion, a little boy about my own age named Jesse, who lived in the house. He sat with me and held my hand and told me the kid would come in the front door with the doctor. I felt sorry for him, for Uncle Ben had told me about childbirth and the sexual relation of men and women. He had told me one cold day when we were on one of our Monday drives. Instead of my hot chocolate at Macgowan's tavern, that day he had ordered me some hot spiced wine. It came, a big pewter beaker of it; one glass raised my spirits to the sky, and he finished the rest. He let the horses have the reins, and we went twice around the reservoir instead of once. I wanted to tell it to Jesse but I could not remember the words he had used. The only words I remembered were that he said now I would know how to take care of myself.

Dr. Bainer had been in the house for hours, only Jesse did not know it. He came out from Mama's room, his coat off, his shirt sleeves rolled up, and a bath towel pinned with safety pins by two of its corners to his vest, and his long white beard was damp.

"You children had better move downstairs another flight where you can see better," he said. His voice was gruff and irritated, but he gave each of my five curls a friendly pull. "Watch good and hard so you don't miss anything. You know we doctors are pretty smart, maybe I'll bring it in another entrance!"

Jesse ran down to the basement door, and I moved down another flight because I could not bear the noises coming from Mama's room. Mama had had a nurse for the past two weeks, a wonderful Englishwoman named Pace. I was stiff and cold from sitting on the stairs when Pace came out to tell me I had a sister. "Red and skinny," said Pace, "but a darling if ever I saw one, a little angel if they 'ave the sense to keep Pace to care for 'er."

Daddy came out of the room wiping his eyes and smiling. "Yes," he sang, "Hit ain't the miles that makes a feller weary, Hit's the 'Ammer 'Ammer 'Ammer on the 'ard 'ard road."

I thought she would be angry, but she seemed to like it and gave him a flick with the towel she had in her hand. Daddy used to tease her about her name. "Fine name for a nurse," he said, "the Pace that kills." She had been trying to bring me up those two weeks she had been with us; little girls should knock on doors before entering, she said, and curtsy to their elders. I never would bend my knee in a curtsy I told her, not to the President of the United States, and as for my parents, after you sit in their laps and sleep in their beds how could you curtsy to them?

But I liked her. She was plain and straight and firm, and bony as a herring. She wore dull jet jewelry when she went out and had a snowy ruching inside her widow's bonnet and she creaked with starch when she was on duty. She was English for ever, as non-absorbent to anything foreign as a block of steel; and she was one of those women who seem to be widowed for ever. They don't exist any more, maybe since the decline of mourning.

My friend Jesse had been taught to read, and he used to read to me. From one of his story books he read me that Mary Queen of Scots had been beheaded. I did not know at first the meaning of the word, but when I did, I could not believe it. I told him it was impossible that one person could kill another, and I had a gory picture of a man hacking at a woman's neck with a small kitchen knife. It was sickening.

"Can't they, though?" he said. "I'll show you."

He grabbed my arm and pulled me upstairs with him. I thought he was going to get his knife or his mother's scissors and try it out on me. Instead he dragged me into my room and took my doll Bessie that was always lying on my pillow. Bessie had a wax head, blue eyes, and turquoise earrings. He put Bessie's head on the window sill and hacked at her neck with his penknife, just like my vision.

"See," he screamed.

The head fell crashing below, and I hated him.

Heads being cut off and people killing one another weighed on my mind day and night. I was afraid to ask Mama about it; if it was not true I did not want to put it into her head and worry her; so I asked one of the chambermaids if it was possible that one person could kill another.

"Why, of course," said Bridget; "what do you think is them things in front of Flanagan's store with the little suits on them, but young ones that's been bad and told lies and had their heads cut off, and their hands too, for taking what wasn't theirs."

I believed her, even after I knew it wasn't true. For there were the little figures standing out on the sidewalk, with the little suits on, and big price marks on their bosoms, their pitiful empty sleeves trembling with the least gust of wind, shoes and stockings painted on their poor dead legs. My life was poisoned. I had a deadly fear that I might be telling a lie without knowing it, I thought so carefully before answering a question that people began to think me stupid, and I tried in every way to evade a direct answer. I ate only what was absolutely necessary for fear I would take something that was not mine by right. I even stopped playing with Nana's jewelry when I went to visit her, for fear the Lord would think I was stealing it. I grew thin and languid and they dosed me with sulphur and molasses. Daddy knew there was something on my mind; he asked me and I broke down and told him. He took me up to Flanagan's himself and showed me the papier-mâché

41

under the clothing. Poor stupid Bridget was discharged, but it took months for the horror to fade and the pink to come back to my cheeks. I was so happy to be able to walk on Eighth Avenue again, and to go to Flanagan's store, which I adored. It was a small department store, almost like a store in a small town, and they had everything for sale. It was a splendid place to spend the quarter that my Cousin Fred gave me every Sunday, and I soon had a drawerful of lovely and useless things.

Nana used to come up to the boarding-house for lunch, she could not get off for dinner, and it was seldom she could persuade Uncle Ben to dine there. But of all the places we ever lived I never loved any so much as that house. Aunt Mamie made a big success of it, she had to turn people away. When the house next door came on the market for rent, she took it and doubled her space. That too was soon filled. An arch was cut in the wall of the front hall, for a connecting passage, and a larger one in the dining-room, throwing the two rooms together. It was a fine sight to see all the people eating their dinners at night, the gaslight making it brighter than day, and all the talk making it fine and loud. There was one long table in the room at 217, and smaller ones in the new room. Aunt Mamie carved and served everything from the head of the long table. She ladled out soup into deep plates from a huge steaming tureen, then she served the fish, then the roast. She flourished the big carving knife like the wand of a drum major. Slice, slice, slice, her diamond rings and diamond earrings twinkling in the gaslight with every movement. She put a good big piece of meat on the top plate of the stack beside her, and her husband, Uncle Sol, followed it up with the gravy, potatoes and vegetables, and in a minute the waitress had her black tin tray loaded with dishes. Everyone sent back his plate for a second helping. Little bits of meat from the roast fell into the dish gravy on the platter, and those were the pieces I liked most. I sat next to her, and after everyone else was served she let me fish out those wonderful morsels for myself. Maybe if I had not been so fond of food the whole colour of my life would have been different.

Aunt Mamie was a strong woman, worldly-wise and determined. She managed the boarding-house so that it paid, and every one of the boarders felt he was lucky to live there. And they were, they had far more comfort and pleasure than they would have had in their own homes. The meals were splendid, the house was clean as wax, and the atmosphere was always gay and pleasant. Aunt Mamie's weakness was the poker table. She played every night, no inducement could take her away from her own card game. It was her reward after her hard day of work, and I think she had a perfect vocation, for there were always seven or eight people living in the house who wanted to play after dinner. Where else could she have found that?

As soon as dinner was over, everyone went into the parlour while the dining-room was cleared up. When it was ready, the head waitress called them. One of the round tables was covered with its tight stretched green felt and the chips were laid out. I was as eager for the game as Aunt Mamie herself; there was always a gallery watching; I ran around the table and looked at everyone's hands, feeling I could play better than any of them. About nine o'clock Mama would say: "Al, you had better think about going to bed," and I would say: "Yes, Mama, I'm thinking about it." But I never went until Delia came in with her tray of food, plates of sandwiches, a pitcher of foaming draught beer, and a bowl of Uncle Sol's dill pickles. He made those pickles in the back yard in a wooden barrel, and they were the best I ever tasted except some that a stage hand once gave me. I was doing a show at the Booth Theatre, and one night during the intermission of a rehearsal an old fellow who was standing in the wings next to me said: "Say, would you like a Jew pickle? A Jew lady showed me how to make them once. I been making them forty years, down cellar in whatever house I'm working." Maybe it was Aunt Mamie showed him. Stranger things have happened, for they tasted just the same.

By skilful manœuvring I managed to stay up pretty late, sometimes until the end. I always heard Aunt Mamie's voice say, as I went up the stairs: "Just one more round, folks, all jack pots." Maybe children nowadays lead too regular a life. I learned a great deal that I never should have known if I had gone to bed early.

I went to market every day with her. She selected every piece of food that came to her table. It was a long serious business, she even picked out each egg; she looked at their colour and felt their weight, holding them up against the light to see, she told me, if there were any chickens in them, because she did not want more than her money's worth. Mr. Lunn, eggs, butter, teas, and coffees, had a store on Eighth Avenue round the corner. Out front was a giant egg, a snow-white egg in a royal-blue cup, as tall as a man. It was a symbol of bigness and whiteness, a goal for every little egg to reach in its career. Inside the shop all the coffees were in black japanned tin boxes along the walls. While Aunt Mamie was looking at the eggs, I raised the lid of a bin and slid my hands in and out among the coffee beans. The satin smooth beans sliding over my hands and through my fingers were a hypnotic rhythm and sensation, and the smell of the coffee from the grinding machine tickled my nose.

Mr. Christopher, the butcher, had his store farther on the avenue on the corner of Forty-fifth Street. Walking up the street Aunt Mamie always took my hand. She wore lace fingerless gloves, called mitts, and her diamond rings shone beautifully through the black threads. As I held her hand I fingered the rings and longed for some of my own.

"I was thinking about ducks for tonight—how does that strike you?" she asked, giving my hand a shake. And immediately I saw and tasted the morsels floating at the bottom of the platter, rich and buttery, fresh, crisp and crackling skin. I rubbed my cheek against her fingers.

"How are ducks today, Mr. Christopher?"

"Nicely, m'am, and lamb is nicely too."

My heart sank, for I never could bear lamb. I did not like the lamby way it tasted, and it always was too closely associated with Jesus. The servant girls had religious pictures plastered all over their bedroom walls. He was either a lamb Himself or had one clutched close to His bosom. Mr. Christopher went into his ice room and came out with six elegant white ducks. "Straight from Long Island, Mrs. Davis, the only place they can raise a duck to suit a táble like yours, so young and tender you could broil 'em. How about the shiksers? What will we give them to eat today, some liver? Some neck of beef? Some corn beef?"

I went out to the sidewalk to avoid the disembowelling of the ducks, and told Aleck, the vegetable man, what we were going to have. Too bad, I said to him, that nothing goes with ducks like cabbage with corn beef. Applesauce, he said, and gave me a banana to eat. But my favourite place was Carstens', the grocer's, even better than Mr. Lunn's. It was a delicious mass of everything, it was dingy and spicy and dark. There were little kegs of gherkins and dill pickles and pickled onions, large tin canisters with open lids of every kind of crackers, sugar wafers, saltines, sultanas, animal crackers and gingersnaps, so you could put your hand in and take one, wonderful white grapes from Spain in a barrel of sawdust, and sacks of rice and beans. Everything was right out to touch and look at, and taste and smell, and there is nothing like it today.

Jesse was my only young companion; otherwise I liked being with the family, the boarders, and the servant girls. Jesse and I had reached a stage of embattled friendship. We fought, and our fights gave the day a brightness and a stimulating tone. A good quarrel is not a bad thing for children, it improves the circulation and helps get rid of a lot of bad coin. It is the aftermath that makes quarrels bitter, the misery of a remembered word, hurt pride, the sore left by the probe of truth, by the enemy's discovery of one's dearest faults. But we never brooded, we never remembered who called whom what, and always went to bed on the best of terms. He slept in just such a little bedroom as mine, down the other end of the hall, and we kept our doors open at night, for we were both inclined to be frightened; it was comforting.

He taught me to read, and before I knew it I was able to read the newspaper. It made little sense to me, the way a lot of the talk I heard made no sense, but the recognition of words in print was exciting. What I saw on the page in letters rang a bell, and the look of the syllables made sound in my ears. Sometimes the sound was not right; "weapon" sounded like "weepon," and "hotel" had a short first syllable like "total," and "misled" had the accent on the first syllable and sounded to me like "drizzled." I read more than Jesse did, but he was the leader, he had the ideas for play. The rubber balls we used to play stoop ball and jackstones were hollow, with a tiny pin-hole in them. Jesse filled them with water and said it would be a fine idea if we went up to his mother's room and squirted water on the people in the street as they passed under the window. We gave them a sporting chance for we only squirted on men who wore grey derby hats. They were all the style that year, and about one man in four wore one.

A gentleman named de Wolfe lived across the way. We did not care for him; he did not like children and found fault with everything we did. He was known in the neighbourhood as Nosy de Wolfe. He saw us squirting water on the passers-by, so he came across the street to report. He was a stylish old fellow and wore a fine new grey derby, so we both let him have it. He probably thought we would not dare to do it to him, seeing he was coming up our own front stoop. Before he had a chance to ring the bell, we beat it up to the roof through the trapdoor on the top floor. We ran over the roofs down the block toward Eighth Avenue, and I went down into the house where the tarts lived. The trapdoor on their roof was always unlocked and I had often gone in that way. Our laundress's sister worked there, so I could always say I came to see her. I went through the house and out the basement door, not meeting a soul. I sauntered up the street, and came up to the house as Mr. de Wolfe was talking to Aunt Mamie at the front door.

"Why, there she is," said Aunt Mamie, holding out her hand to me. "She was down the block all the time. I knew you must be mistaken, Mr. de Wolfe, my little darling would never do a thing like that."

"Like what?" I asked, with wide eyes.

Aunt Mamie motioned me into the house before I could spoil it by overacting. She knew there was something phony. I went into the parlour and through the thick lace curtains watched Mr. de Wolfe cross the street. His back was bent, sad, and old, and I was sorry. His daughter was sitting in the second-floor front window, looking at a flower she had in her hand. He came to the window and spoke to her, but I could see she did not answer, she kept looking at the flower. She was beautiful in an unearthly way, thin, pale, and dark-haired, dressed always in too many white floating garments. She had a white poodle dog, and when the old father died, she dressed all in black and got a black poodle. Daddy said she played only on the black keys of the piano, but his eyes wrinkled. He could not help saying things like that.

Two tarts lived in that house down the block near Eighth Avenue. They were mother and daughter. They were pretty as pictures, all lightness and lace.

Their appearance was so different from so-called respectable women, they might have belonged to another race. They wore only what was pretty, nothing that was only useful, even when they bundled up to go out in the cold. Neither of them ever set foot on a sidewalk except to step into a carriage. They drove out every afternoon about three o'clock, in a victoria if it was fine, in a brougham if it rained. Even in winter they went out in their open carriage when the sun shone, wrapped in wonderful blond furs. They drove around the park, stopped at Macgowan's Pass for a drop of something, then home for late afternoon visitors. I saw them at the Pass once when I was with Uncle Ben, but they did not remember me. Nobody at home knew I went there, or knew about the trapdoor on the roof. They never went out in the daytime except for those drives, never went shopping, the shops came to them. Milliners and dressmakers came with masses of things to choose from, their shoemaker came and measured and fitted them for their dozens of pairs of shoes and slippers. They were the only women I knew except Nana who wore high French heels on their daytime shoes.

They looked so much alike, and so near an age to my eye, that they might have been sisters. The mother, Flora, was in command. She was stronger-looking, and although they were both decidedly blonde, she had a tawnier colouring and a healthier build. It was in her rooms that the dresses and goods were always spread out. She had the entire second floor, front and back, and the young one, Miss Ella, had the third floor. Flora kept house and kept it beautifully, as exquisite a place as you ever saw; it smelled as sweet as a lilac bush after a rain. There was a glint of gold all over the house, and Miss Ella was the most golden of all—her hair, her eyes, and her skin. Her rooms were in cream satin and gold, with lace falling all over the edges like foam on the crest of a wave. On a table in every room in the house was a deep covered crystal dish, filled with finger-shaped pieces of pineapple, that Miss Ella ate when she was hungry. Our laundress told me that her sister said that Miss Ella never sat down to a proper meal. She ate pineapple all day, and while the gentlemen were there at night she had chicken salad brought up to her rooms, along with what the gentlemen wanted to eat. She drank champagne when she was thirsty, no matter when. A coloured boy lived with them, he had a room down off the kitchen and tended to the drinks and serving things.

I saw more of Ella than of Flora; she did not seem to be so busy during the day. Ella called me in when

she heard me on the stairs. She said she liked to look
at me and talk to me, and she offered me pieces of
her fruit, dipping it out of the deep dish with her
ridiculous useless hand, so thin, so soft, so boneless.
She did not like my plaid dresses and said she would
give me a nice cream cashmere made by her own
dressmaker, Mme McCarthy. She could not understand my aunt letting me dress that way. I told her
Mama made all my things and it was nobody else's
say-so. They did not seem to mind that I came in and
out as I did, but Flora used to look at me in an odd
way and say I should not come after five. She rarely
spoke to me except one day when Ella sent me down
to her room with a message. Ella was in bed, under
the weather she told me, and she wanted Flora to
come up and look at a present a friend from Chicago
had sent her.

I knocked at Flora's door and she called to me to
come in. Her room was different from Ella's, much
less light; it had velvet curtains of sapphire blue, and
the dressing-table had no lace, it was made of mot-
tled onyx and brass. She was sitting before it as I
came in, looking into her eyes, and combing her curly
bangs over her eyebrows with a thin tortoise-shell
comb. She asked how old I was and why I came into
the house so much and what I was going to do when

I grew up, if I was going on the stage like my father, or if I would like to come and live in a pretty house like theirs some day and have a good time. I said I was going to be one of Shakspere's heroines, and she threw back her head and laughed. There was a blue vein that ran from under her ear down her throat to the collar-bone. I had not noticed it before. It was beautiful on her milky skin, only a shade deeper blue than the pale silk peignoir she wore.

I should have liked to stay and tell her more about what I wanted to do, I should have liked to put out my finger and touch that blue vein, follow it down along the skin that I knew must be soft as velvet. But I gave her Ella's message, and she said to tell Ella she would be up as soon as she finished doing her hair, and she said to tell Ella she must have been a very good girl indeed to get such a fine expensive present. It *was* an expensive present, a lovely thing; it was a long gold chain to hold her muff—every inch there was a diamond, and two lovely diamond hands clasped each other where the chain joined at the back.

Those two women talked together and laughed a lot; they chattered together like a couple of birds, but I never could make much sense of what they said. I was always under a spell when I was in the house with them, but it was never the excitement I knew with Nana. After a while I grew tired of the scent, and of so much that was pretty; I was glad to get back to the boarding-house to smell Aunt Mamie's good big dinner cooking, and to go down to the kitchen and have a cup of strong black tea with the Irish girls.

Five

"But you're only moving down the block, you silly girl," Aunt Mamie said, giving my hand that little shake, which was so like her, and so affectionate. "You behave as though you would never have a bite to eat again as long as you live."

"It will never be the same," I said, the words catching in my throat, the first glimmering in my heart of the inevitable certainty of change. I was right, it never was the same.

One day Uncle Ben came up to have a long talk with Mama; he said that Nana was going the limit, although he was never to know what Nana's limit could be.

"Beck," he said, and tears were in the eyes of that strong man, who had found the one thing he could not conquer, "you are the only one who can save her; maybe having the children in the house will be good for her. She needs all the love she can get, you know her heart. I'm trying hard to do the best I can. I don't want to be bitter."

Mama telegraphed to Daddy to ask his consent, but she had already made up her mind, and we rented No. 201 down near Broadway. I was sick about leaving the boarding-house; I loved the crowd of people, the splendid loud talk, the poker games, the bright gaslight all over, and the safe feeling that I need never be alone. Even after I had gone to bed, I knew there were people in the dining-room and the parlour, and dozens of them scattered through the house in their own rooms. Each one of them was my friend.

A new regime was started for me, I had to go to bed at regular hours, and we had a real nurse girl, a German girl named Dena. I hated that girl and she hated me. She claimed I was a ruined child before she set foot in the house. I used to look at her and wish she would die right where she was. I used to sit in my chair while she was feeding the baby; apparently I was being a good girl, but all the time I was wishing that her nose would drop off, that her ears would shrivel up, and that I could push her eyes back into the cavity of her head, the way I could push in the eyes of my doll. I raised the heavy earlap of our dog, and whispered in his ear to bite her; but he was too good. He was a beautiful enormous dreamy Saint Bernard; Uncle Ben had bought him to help take care of us. His ears and jowls were pendent masses, his brow was furrowed in a deep design, and his topaz eyes looked sadly at me for asking him to do such a thing. But Dena was wonderful with the baby; when she bathed and dressed her for the night, she dusted her off with sweet powder, put on her little flannel night drawers, and combed the soft yellow baby hair across her head in a golden cock's-comb.

Uncle Ben had his office in the back parlour. Few patients came to the house, he was only in for an hour in the morning, but it gave the house a hushed and formal atmosphere. His brougham waited out in front, and I hoped all the children on the block would see it. Nana never used the carriage except at night when they went to dinner parties, and the time was not far off when they stopped that altogether. Maybe they were no longer invited, or he might not have wanted to run the risk of one of her scenes. She disliked him, she meant to take no part in his life, and was going her way to her own excitements.

Although we all seemed better off financially than ever before, the house had little worries in it. Daddy had a fine engagement in stock at the Lyceum Theatre, a forty-week engagement; Uncle Ben provided liberally for the household and rent, and Nana saw to it that Mama had everything she wanted. Yet there was worry in the air. I began to worry; because I was not so clever as Ruby Jacobs or so pretty as Nancy Harrigan, and I worried because the cook told me maybe no one would marry me when I grew up, because most of them liked yellow hair and blue eyes. I worried because I was afraid that Daddy would be killed by a robber on his way home from the theatre, that Mama might die, and that Nana would run away with the gentleman who lived next door. The girls talked about it in the kitchen, and the thought of it was like a needle sticking in my brain.

This gentleman who lived next door was a good friend to me. In the beginning it was only from hearing about him in the kitchen that I was aware of him at all. Then I noticed something, when I waited in the afternoon for Nana to come in from her walk. She went for her walk every day about three, rain or shine; it was her only discipline, and she did it because it kept her figure firm. I could see her when she came home turn into Forty-fourth Street from the corner of Broadway, walk up the opposite side of the street from our house, walk up the street across the way until she came just opposite our house, then stop a minute to look for wagons or carriages, her fine head turning beautifully from side to side. Before she crossed she lifted her skirts so they would clear the gutter. She was a master at it. She gathered the back of the skirts in her right hand, swirling them forward, so the ruffled lining and frilled silk petticoat showed above her ankles and you could see ten inches of her high-heeled buttoned shoes. She held her pocketbook in her left hand but managed to pick up just a pinch of skirt above her knee with the thumb and forefinger. Holding her skirts that way moulded her thighs and showed every beautiful curve of her figure. As she stepped over the curb to the cobblestones, she raised her eyes to the house next door and I could see a slight tremor come over her, in her eyes and ruffles and the feathers in her hat. If I chanced to be playing outdoors, I might see the lace curtains in the parlour of 203 part, and a hand come through for a brief second. Sometimes she just came swinging up our side of the street, at dusk or later; and if she let me kiss her, her face was warm, and her perfume was tinged with a reek of liquor.

This gentleman's life was caught in two passions: first and foremost a love of art, second the pursuit of pleasure. He rode that passion like a handsome yacht riding a blue and wavy sea; that passion was not only for the ladies, but for food and wine, flowers and rides into the country, and wonderful parties, at Claremont or Delmonico's. He was a fanatic collector and lived under the spell of whatever he was interested in at the time: Chinese porcelains, then American paintings, English eighteenth-century furniture, American furniture, and lastly American colonial paintings. Every one of his collections became famous, and he tired of every one of them and sold them at auction, usually at a handsome profit. Once he started to collect, it was like a disease that had to run its course, and he had an uncanny ability to find what he wanted. He was married to a handsome woman of fine family, who seemed to understand him perfectly and they had a son and a daughter. When I was young and poor and wanted to study and did not know where to turn for help, he sent me to art school. We were a generation apart in age, but there was a great bond between us; not the least was our love of Nana.

He told me that as a child he lived with his parents on Washington Square. His father, who was a scholar, kept a boys' day school in the house in which they lived, one of those noble brick houses on the north side of the square. The boy went to his father's school; after hours he wandered in the late afternoons through old streets, looking at the old houses, wandering aimlessly, looking for new sights and new neighbourhoods. One day he found himself in Chinatown. It was a dark place then, with none of the gaudy restaurants and gilded fronts and tawdry shops of today. It was a few streets where Chinamen huddled together, a place of mystery where a boy might well disappear. He was in a dim narrow street, no wider than an alley; the afternoon was almost gone. He was looking into the window of a basement shop down a few steps from the sidewalk and feeling a little frizzle of fear of the Chinamen going by him in their silent shoes. In the window, among the canisters and painted tea-boxes, the old pewter ducks and fishes and bowls, the pipes and masses of junk, he saw a great china jar. Its ground colour was black, it sparkled like a black diamond; over the surface was a thick pattern of white hawthorn, and in the hawthorn branches were full-throated birds, some flying, some resting in the branches, some singing, with their heads raised; you could hear the song, he said, trilling from their palpitating throats. He told me that he felt he had never seen anything in his life before he saw that jar.

He went into the shop, and it took courage. He jingled the change in his pocket, figuring in his mind how much he had, afraid there was not enough money in New York to buy such a treasure. It was so dark inside that at first he thought the shop was empty. Then he heard a clinking sound. He strained his eyes and saw a Chinaman counting coins at a table in the corner. He was shaking, partly with fear and partly with excitement. He asked the Chinaman if he would sell the jar in the window, and for how much. The man finished his counting before he turned and answered.

"Too dear for boy, seven dollar, cheaper ones here, twenty-fi cent, tirty cent, senty cent," and he pulled aside a dirty curtain showing a long row of shelves, and the boy knew that at the age of fourteen he had found what he wanted. The shelves were crowded with porcelains, stacks of blue and white plates, heaps of blue and white bowls, a row of five blue and white jars in some sort of set, smaller jars and pots of strange shapes and graceful forms, and gorgeous colours; apple green, tea yellow, clair de lune, aubergine, sang de bœuf, and one small jar in the corner that nearly drew his eyes from his head. It was a vase no more than five inches tall, a soft rich glowing pink, a peach-blow.

He didn't know what he was looking at, naturally he had never heard of the great Oriental porcelains, it was even before the time of Mr. Whistler and Mr. Wilde, and it was only years later that he came to know the wonderful descriptive names, beaker and gallipot and garniture, famille rose, soft paste and hard paste, and all the sonorous names of the dynasties.

He bought the little peach-blow for eighty-five cents, all the money he had with him, and mortgaged his life weeks ahead for the hawthorn jar. His allowance was fifty cents a week, and he left one of his gold cuff-buttons with the store-keeper as a deposit. In a year practically all the porcelains he saw that dark afternoon were in his own room. He got two years' allowance in advance, as well as Christmas and birthday money. His parents must have been splendid people, to do that for a boy. "But what did I want with sleds and skates and baseball bats?" and he tapped his lame right leg with the gold-headed cane that never was out of his hand.

Then he began weeding out, selling the least beautiful jars and plates to any of his mother's friends or the boys' parents who would buy, and replaced them with better ones whenever he had the money. He told me he was obsessed. He would get up in the night to touch his treasures, to pass his hands over them in the dark. He was so saturated with his passion for porcelains, so sensitive to their surface, that he could tell the colours by the feel, differences in the pastes and glazes so slight that his ability was magic. At fourteen he founded a business, which helped to create two

of the finest collections of Chinese porcelains in this
country. But he always kept the hawthorn jar as a
talisman.

One day he fell in love with something else, this
time a painting. A friend had taken him to visit
George Inness in his studio, somewhere in Jersey. It
was an October afternoon, smelling of fallen leaves
and bonfires and pumpkins, the autumn mists and
clouds toning the too brilliant red and orange and
gold of the trees into a richness. The painting was a
Grey Lowery Day. In that picture were intensified
the sights and smells of the country he had seen on
the journey down. It held the same divine creative
selection from nature that he had found in the Chinese
porcelains. So he bought it and every picture that was
in Inness's studio that day.

He went to see other men painting, and bought
again; Ryder, Homer, Blakelock, Eakins, Duveneck,
everyone that satisfied his taste. Pictures hung all
over his house, that first year I knew him; pictures on
the walls of the rooms, the halls, up the stairways, on
the landing, and in the bathrooms.

Then he fell in love with Nana. He could not have
known in the beginning what it was going to be like
with Nana. Nobody ever realized her insidious en-
veloping attraction until the time came when it seemed

65

impossible to live without her. Then it was too late.

Some sort of bowing acquaintance grew up between our two households. Mama and his wife, Mrs. Watson, would say how do you do if they met on the street or going up the front stoop of their houses. I wanted to see the pictures and all the other things in that crowded house. Our waitress had told me about them, she had been listening to complaints from their waitress, who said it was impossible to keep the place clean; and people were in and out all hours of the day and night looking at the things, tracking up the halls and stairs and having to be let in when she was taking forty winks in the afternoon. I hung around the sidewalk waiting for Mrs. Watson to come along, then I asked her one day if I might come in. It was wonderful.

There was not an inch of space on a wall without a picture. I guess it was the wrong way to show pictures, but it suited me. I could look at one as long as I liked, then go on to another. There were glass cases in the parlour with Chinese porcelains, and one case with those lovely Greek terracotta figurines from Tanagra. In the dining-room over the mantel hung the *Grey Lowery Day*. There were the beautiful rich-coloured trees, like port wine and Moselle and sherry; there were sodden clouds and silver sky, patches of

66

green on the olive ground and a small red building in the distance. That picture made me feel many things; first I felt the sad hopeful stimulation I feel on a cool rainy day in the autumn; then I felt things not represented in the picture at all. I would think of being in Mama's arms at night, or in the kitchen in the afternoon when Amelia made cake, or getting into a steaming hot bath with the good unperfumed clean smell of Pears' soap, and it made me think of that wonderful time at night when everybody was home, when I knew Daddy had come in from the theatre and I could turn around and go to sleep, safe.

Mr. Watson came home that afternoon while I was there. He had his own hansom cab, and I heard the peculiar noise that only a hansom makes; the horse stops, four feet planted firm, but the cab is still pro-pelled by its own weight, and you hear the shafts grinding. Then you hear the apron doors open and when the cab is empty they bang shut again, and the horse starts up by pawing the cobbles with his two front feet, then a jump forward and a rattle of doors and wheels.

I heard the front door open and close, and his un-even step, his cane tapping on the marble floor of the hall. I had never spoken to him before, and when he came into the room where I had been looking at the picture I was frightened and embarrassed. He handled himself and his lameness wonderfully; once he came into a room, he moved slowly and almost imperceptibly to where he wanted to be, and he stayed there, so that he would not disturb people with his painful walk. He stood a great deal, his hand always resting on the gold crook of his cane; it was a splendid white hand, and on the third finger he wore an enormous intaglio ring, an emerald carved with a boy and a goat, set in a lump of yellow gold.

He was pure blond, so rare in a man, gold hair and white skin; his eyes were sapphire blue and always sparkling and there was sweetness and humour in the curve of his mouth, particularly in the deep corners. Behind the mask of his face you felt there was a big private good time going on.

"How did you get in, young lady?" he said, and when he spoke to me I felt that was the way to speak to people who liked to look at pictures. "You seem to like it."

We both looked up at the painting, and I said: "It makes me think—it makes me think—" but I could not finish, for how did he know what it was like to smell the ginger cake come out of the pans, or know that wonderful sinking into bliss from fear that I knew at night?

68

He limped a step nearer, looking down into my eyes.

"That is what a painting should be," he said. Then he asked me if I wanted to be an artist, and for the moment I forgot about Shakspere and said yes. Saturday morning a box of roses came for Nana, and a box for me. There were Windsor and Newton's moist water-colours in a black japanned box, a china palette, a sable brush, and a pad of rough water-colour paper.

Six

Things had started well with us in 201, but they were not keeping up. At first everybody was happy because Nana was not taking so much of her drugs, she was far more natural, and her gaiety was not so feverish, not so likely to sink into a ditch of melancholy afterwards. Daddy was having a splendid season, but he began to have little quarrels with Mama, and it grew later and later at night when I heard the front door close and the jingle of his key-ring as he put it back into his pocket. Sometimes he did not come home at all between the matinee and evening performances on Saturdays, and one Saturday he brought home a girl from the company for dinner. There was a lot of thick atmosphere at the table, and Uncle Ben looked like thunder. The estrangement between Uncle Ben and Nana had reached such a point that they made no show at all of friendliness to each other. His lower jaw was always pushed forward in anger and it gave his

70

beard a fiery thrust like a burning bush. Nana never looked handsomer and came out with the most beautiful clothes. But Uncle Ben was awful. He had loved me like his own, and now he barely spoke to me. It was a cruel way to behave to a child. I did not know then what I was seeing, but it was my first sight of the foul monster jealousy, and its mate, injustice.

Mama was worn out with worry, and I think it would have made her sick only that we went away for a while in the spring. I don't know how she ever brought herself to leave Nana, but I believe that she had an idea it would be better for them to be left alone together to work things out. Daddy's company was going on the road for about six weeks with some of their New York successes, and I heard her say to Aunt Mamie that his salary might as well be spent on us instead of running into drinks and jamborees for the company. But she was worried about him I know, and the girl called Aggie who had come for dinner that night. Dena and the baby were left behind and I was so happy to be going that I forgot to hate Dena.

The road was hard work, and you could not blame the actors for going on the spree. The tension needed some relief. They put up night after night at cheap boarding-houses or station hotels, that all smelt of musty carpets, fried food, and slops; and often after the show at any old time there was a train, sometimes at two or three in the morning. We travelled in a day coach to the next stop, arriving cold and weary in a dirty grey town at dawn. Only the long jumps had sleepers, and even then if business had been poor we had to use the day coaches. Rehearsals were called in the forenoon, for we were doing repertory. There were no Ritzes in Boston or Philadelphia for us, no ladies' clubs and tony social parties. A split week in a couple of nice towns seemed like heaven. Sometimes we got into a town in the afternoon, then there was only time for a snack before the performance and we had our chief meal after the show. I had to be taken along because I couldn't be left alone in whatever strange places we were living at; so I ate my steak and drank a little glass of beer with the rest of them. It was an irregular life, and the odd meals at odd times, the night air, the bad weather, the snatches of sleep, and the long night journeys made me tough and strong.

Our little life was a world; and the sun of that world was our star. He ruled us with an iron rod tipped with a sharp steel spike. Acting was more than just walking on the stage and being yourself; you had to be prepared to play any character, young or old, and speak your lines so that every letter of every syllable of every word could be heard in the last row of the gallery and emotion had to be expressed in no uncertain terms. The actors were the darlings of the gallery, and from that heaven came the heart-warming whistles and shouts and foot-stamping and hand-clapping; or alas sometimes the reverse. They had to have voices, and they did, rich and fruity, with tones like an organ. They practised, Daddy practised on his voice every day as a pianist does five-finger exercises. He walked up and down the room doing m's and ng's and moo's, and the sound wound through his head like a horn; he finished up with a mighty sentence: "Praise be the Lord," over and over again, louder and louder, until his voice resounded back from the walls, musical and strong.

I rarely slept in a proper bed on tour; it would be a cot or a hard plush sofa or a seat on the train with my head in Mama's lap. I learned to fight sleep, not to do without it, but to sleep when I could. I bit the inside of my cheeks, I twisted my foot around my ankle so the pain kept me awake, I held my eyes open with my forefingers. Then when I could sleep, it was the most wonderful sleep of all—it became a luxury, a reward, instead of an accepted part of life that one never noticed. If we travelled at night, we checked out of wherever we were living before the performance, in order to save the night's rent, and Mama and I spent the eve-

ning in the theatre. I visited around in the dressing-
rooms; nobody seemed to mind it. Sometimes I took
a nap. There was a large green plush armchair that
was used in the last act of one of the plays. It had a
deep seat and enormous spreading arms, and had the
smell of the theatre; grease paint and that footlight
smell that is like a thunderstorm. I loved to take a little sleep in that chair. The property man covered me
up with a piece of shawl and woke me up when he
came to set the scene. But one night there was a slip,
and I woke up on the stage. A violin was sobbing and
a lovely lady stood by the fireplace. She wore a white
dress with a long ruffled train and all her edges were
coloured with the ruby light from the grate fire. One
hand was pressed to her heart, and the other extended
in a sweeping gesture toward the leading man. "And
have you forgotten Étretat and those days of love?" he
was saying up to the gallery. And her velvet voice answered: "Leave me, Bellamy, me heart can bear no
more."

The chair was below the fireplace and turned up-
stage, so I guess the house could not see me in the
shadow. I scarcely breathed, for I knew her next move
was to sit on that chair and give way to grief. There
was a pause, and I knew what the actor was doing, I
had seen it often; he would drop his chin on his chest,

74

pick up his high silk hat, flick his knee with his white kid glove, take in the audience with a look, and go off stage with halting, grief-stricken feet. Then she crossed over slowly, a hand pressed to her throat, and there was a pause as she too gave the audience a look, assuring them of her virtue and her sacrifice. I was scared stiff that she would sit down without noticing me, but she did notice the object in the chair and steeled herself. Our eyes met. "God, Joe's infant," came under her breath, but it was drowned by the shivering music. I shrank, I melted into the plush, and in all her loveliness she finished the scene leaning against the mantelpiece.

Nothing finds you out quicker than the theatre. Your quality is tested, your ability to work, and your reaction to necessity. You have to develop a steely strength, not so much against your weaknesses as against the intrusion of your weaknesses upon the professional life. Between midnight and rehearsal call, your life is your own, and you can go to hell if you get back in the theatre in time. I've seen them do it, both men and women, and they always lose out in the end. I've seen a man so drunk that night after night he was barely able to stand straight in the wings, yet I've seen him go on and give a sober performance. That can't keep up for ever, but it can be done; and on the other hand I have seen a woman play three acts of a comedy coming straight from her child's deathbed. When an actor comes on the stage, he is no longer himself, he has escaped the bonds of his own life, and magic takes place. Unfortunately there are bad actors.

Mama was enjoying herself in spite of her concern about Nana being in New York without her. Nana was no writer, but she would catch us once in a while with a letter that was just like her.

"The baby is all right, Dena is looking sour, Bregney made a botch of my blue grenadine and it has to go into the rag bag. Hollander is making me a toque of coq feathers that is going to be beautiful with my green cloth princess. Betty is sick every morning and cries if you talk to her. It looks like trouble to me, and it is that Cousin Harry of hers or I'm a Dutchman. It is getting warmer and lots of victorias are out in the park. There is some talk of taking up the cobblestones on Forty-fourth Street and putting down asphalt, but I guess that will be a long time away. It's too hard on the horses in the winter. Mrs. Hitchcock got drunk last night and locked her daughter out, the whole block leaning out the window to hear what they called each other. Take care of yourself, Beck, and have a good time, and for God's sake *don't worry*."

There was nothing about herself, or her own domestic matters, only about her clothes.

I loved the life, I even liked the discomforts. I enjoyed being part of a group. It made me feel slightly delirious when we waited on the platform of the station for the night train. Daddy and one of the other actors would stage shows, fake quarrels which I liked to fancy were real. One would edge close or jostle or step on a toe or swing a can and catch the other on the shin. An apology was demanded, it was denied, the quarrel started, grew hot, and then the fight. Canes were used like swords, terrific and dramatic; they went so far as to knock each other down. Then remorse and belated apologies, vows of friendship, fraternal kisses on either cheek, the platform pacing resumed, but arm in arm, and singing. I could transport myself into the reality of those quarrels, even tried at times to interfere.

I never grew tired of the company, nor watching the shows from the wings, and watching the actors make up. Some grease paint, a few lines, a wig, and a man made himself into someone else. I thought it was a wonderful way to spend a life and decided that I would be a great actress. It was splendid to think that I could take on another skin and have another self. Our star let me stay in his dressing-room whenever I wanted. We were doing four plays, but what I liked best was to watch him make up for *Richard III.* He was a glamorous man, handsome, and had a slight foreign accent that was charming with a smouldering deep nature. It was fascinating to see his beautiful face grow hideous, the features distorted, the clammy ugly colour, the mauve lips, the dark hair in ugly strands straggling over his collar, the hump on his back, and the crooked shoulder. But the final touch, the stroke of the master, came when he left his dressing-room and became bloody Richard. Between his room and the wings he fell into the horrid hunchback's walk, a short step and a lope, a short step and a lope, and that gait held all of Richard's lustful senseless cruelty. While he stood waiting to go on, I could not look into his face, for I knew he was not himself, and I was afraid of what I saw.

Two girls played the young princes. One day the smaller one sprained her ankle and could not go on. It was about an hour before curtain time; fortunately we had all had our supper and were in the theatre. I said I could play the prince if they would let me. I knew the entire show, the words and the business, I could have gone on and done Richard in my fashion. They let me do it; the wardrobe mistress pulled up the tights around my waist and sewed me into the black velvet jerkin that was too large. I always wanted to be a blonde, and I had a lovely blond club wig. Our star made me up himself. He put me in a chair in front of him, held my chin in his left hand and with his right hand he rouged my cheeks with the rabbit's foot from his own rouge-pot. He held his mascara tin over the candle and lengthened my eyelashes one by one, although he said they scarcely needed it. He called me his bit of luck, and as I looked into his face I had to close my eyes because I was dazzled. I was so happy I could feel the smile widen on my face so it nearly cut a circle round my head. My one sadness was that Nana was not there to see me and share my excitement. She was so wonderful about things, and I am sure she would have had my picture taken, which nobody else thought about doing.

We only played *Richard* in the larger towns, so I did not go on often; besides, the young lady soon got well again; but I found out how to do it, how to lose myself, how to attach myself to an image. No matter how life went, I could never be robbed of that. All of us wanted the same thing, we wanted to do our stuff, to tell our story. You try to sit down in a room and tell somebody what it is like to be blue, sad, lonely, frustrated, unfulfilled, tell somebody what it is like to feel gay and bright and want the moon and think you are going to get it, and you will bore him to death. But get up on the stage, put on your sable coat and your plumes, your tarlatan and your spangles, speak the words and act the actions not of your ordinary sorrow or joy, but the words and actions of drama. Look, and see them weep and laugh. It was only right that such magicians as ourselves should be marked from other people. Let them pay their price to see us, up on our platform at our privileged angle.

The tour was successful, the whole country wanted to see our great actor, and we ended with a brilliant week in Philadelphia. He longed for more worlds to conquer. On the way home to New York in the train he announced that he would go to London for a season, take the entire company and productions, and show the English what the best American theatre was like.

My heart sank. It meant a long time without Daddy. It was not only that I loved him and would miss him, but now that this acting business had happened, he meant more to me than ever. While we were gone, something must have happened between Nana and her friend next door. She was on more friendly terms with Uncle Ben, they talked to each other, and when she came home from her afternoon walks she turned down the block from Broadway on our side.

I do not know whose idea it was, but it was arranged

that all of us including Dena and the baby, should go to Europe. It must have been Uncle Ben, for there was so much money involved. He and Nana were going ahead of us to Switzerland, then take a tour, and would meet us in London.

It was too good to be true, but it was true, and we sailed with the company on the *City of Rome,* Anchor Line, locking the front door of 201 and leaving Betty, married by now, and blissful in the basement, with her cousin from the navy.

Seven

We had lodgings in London on Torrington Square. We stayed overnight in Liverpool and came up to London on a day of unbelievable wetness. It was not so much that it was raining but that the moisture from all over oozed and enveloped everything. London was slate grey, and if it had not been for the new sights, I would have cried with homesickness and disappointment. Everything was different from what I had imagined. I had seen an engraving of the Colosseum and I thought the good ship *City of Rome* would be a series of openwork archways, with the company and crew threading in and out like a pageant. I expected to see willowy aristocrats on the street, like the Du Maurier drawings I loved in *Punch,* the men in evening dress and flowing Dundreary whiskers, the ladies in basques and fabulous bustles, with their front hair frizzled and the most exquisite grace of bearing. I was to find that later, but at first the people on the street looked like the people on the Bowery, only with less colour and very, very drab. Our first meal was a lovely English tea, laid on our sitting-room table, seed cake, citron cake, and sponge cake, strawberry jam and blackberry jam, boiled eggs and toasted crumpets, and the huge teapot had a red satin quilty cozy, the first I ever saw. It took the curse off that rainy day, and within a week we loved London.

As always, I longed for Nana to share every experience. I enjoyed things twice, once for myself alone and again through her. They were coming soon, but as I knew London better, our cousins and the people we met, I was a little doubtful of Nana in London. In my heart I felt disloyal to think so, but she was the very flavour of New York.

We were a pleasant surprise to our English relations. The one I liked was Cousin Julia. She was a writer, and I thought that if I could be like her, I would give up the idea of being a great actress. She was superbly tailored until tea-time, and then every afternoon she received in lovely tea gowns. Hers was the first really beautiful house I ever saw. It was a perfect Georgian house, everything in it had beauty and order; the design of the furniture, the chintz, the arrangement of flowers, the way food was passed at table, and the tea service. It was brilliantly clean, the silver and old woods looked as though they not only had just been polished, but had been polished for hundreds of years.

She invited me to stay with her for a week, and it was a treat for me to sit in her beautiful drawing-room and talk to the visitors. It was like a story, an elegant and beautiful interpretation of ordinary life. It was the sort of thing I always hoped to see when I went to the theatre. At first I did not understand what people said, it was like a foreign language, but as my ear grew accustomed to the intonation and I understood the words, if not always the meaning, I found the speech had the same style and beauty as the room itself.

The first day Cousin Julia asked me to come in for tea, she was sitting on the sofa talking to an old gentleman with a long white beard. Miss Pinkney, who was her own children's governess, thought it odd, for their children never came into the drawing-room for tea. They all lived upstairs like a separate little family, almost like a lot of little lepers, it seemed to me. Miss Pinkney was awfully good to me, she brushed my hair until it shone like burnished metal, she dressed me in my brown velveteen with the wide lace collar that was made like Lord Fauntleroy's suit, and the long brown silk stockings and bronze slippers that Nana had sent me from Paris.

I was sitting on a hassock drawn up close to the sofa

so that I would not miss a word they said, enjoying my tea, a pale spicy cupful, so different from the strong black brew that I used to have with the servant girls in Aunt Mamie's kitchen. She was telling the old gentleman that she had invited me to stay with her so she could find out something about America. "So far," she said, "the visit has been a success."

I asked her what she thought we would be like. "I guess you thought I would carry a tommyhawk," I said, and she laughed as she lit up another of her endless cigarettes.

"Yes, I was afraid of you, you know, it is the gossip here that American children carry those what-do-you-call-'ems, and I thought Joe would wear a red flannel shirt with pistols and knives stuck around his belt, and I thought your dear Mama would wear a sunbonnet right in to tea."

She leaned over and ran her forefinger through one of my curls. "And I thought you would have two horns and a tail and a very dirty nose." She kept running her finger through my hair, then she took my chin in her hand and turned my face to the old gentleman. "It might be a pleasant place to visit," she said to him.

"You'd love it," I said, "if only you could come at election time when we have our bonfires, and I think

you would like to live at Aunt Mamie's boarding-
house, there's a poker game every night, and something is always going on. Just wait until you see Nana!"
But as I spoke, I doubted Nana in Cousin Julia's beautiful room, and again I had that unpleasant ache of
secret disloyalty.

Daddy was a great personal success among the profession. He was put up at the Garrick Club and invited
everywhere. He had to buy a lot of new clothes, for he
said he had to wear the clothes every day and evening
that he only wore to funerals and weddings at home.
Some of his invitations included Mama, some did not,
but she said they had to take her in her handsome black
silk or not at all; but she ripped the lace yoke out of
her bodice and bought a feather thing to wear in her
hair. It was all expensive, it cost as much again as they
had to spend, but as Daddy pointed out, it was good,
and Mama said: "We can't economize, we must increase our income."

The company rehearsed four weeks, which was a lot
considering how long they had played together. Our
star wanted perfection, in acting and production. I
often went to rehearsal; he worked the actors until
they were ready to drop, and worked himself into a
frenzy. He had no pity, and often at the end of a trying
day there were horrible scenes. He accused them of

everything it was worst to accuse an actor of; and every day he picked on one individual to be the butt of his temper. He once went so far as to hit one of his best actors with a prop sword, and that day there was mutiny in the cast. That was the way he worked, and I never found out if he really had that ungovernable temper or if it was designed to get the best out of them. He opened with his wonderful Richard, and it was a failure.

He should have been smart enough to know it. The English had their own Shaksperian traditions and resented the intrusion of anything so foreign. The critics claimed they could not understand the American actors, which I believed, because we could not understand them, at first. Our productions had more life and beauty, our scenery and costumes were better, and we had a fresher pace. They did not like that, either. Our failure was a blow, and nearly robbed me of my enjoyment of London.

I loved it so; the noble Georgian houses and the huge gloomy Victorian houses, the leafy squares and the crescents, and the horsy smell of the mews. I loved the cries of the venders, the shining pots of milk and cream on the handcarts, flowers in the window boxes all around our square, and flowers to buy from the girls on the streets with their full baskets. You could buy a big bunch of sweet violets for a penny. I had a governess. She taught me the three R's, and French conversation, drawing, needlework, and the finest Spencerian penmanship; and I was soon speaking London English, which made me fancy myself a great deal.

Nana and Uncle Ben finished their tour and came to London for the opening of our company. She looked superb. The trip must have done her good, but I heard her tell Mama that the only part of it she liked was Paris, and she said that some day before she died she wanted to go back there with the right company.

"You can keep your Switzerland and Germany," she said. "I had enough scenery to last the rest of my life. I must give it credit, it helped to keep my mind off other things. But Paris! Beck, I couldn't look out of the corner of my eye but what there was a row; and what good would it have done me anyway if someone did speak to me, when I couldn't speak a word of the language? He should have known that."

"Still," said Mama, "he must have been pretty decent to you."

Nana was unpacking her trunks, and her new things were spread all over the room; lots of dresses, and silk petticoats, and underwear that was so full of lace and ribbons that you couldn't see a bit of muslin. While she was talking to Mama she had put a long feather boa around her neck, it was a fluffy rope that reached the ground on both sides. She gave herself a nod of admiration as she looked at her effect in the long glass. I caught her eye, and we both laughed. We knew we were looking at something mighty fine. It was wonderful to have her back with us, to hear the rustle of her silks, and to smell the clean fresh orris with which all her things were scented. I began to understand something of Uncle Ben's suffering at the thought of losing her, and to know the hundred ways she devilled him, and to realize that it was not only children who suffered.

Once more he took me out and bought me presents. He bought me a life-size doll that cost a fortune and I hated it, and bananas that were terribly expensive, sixpence apiece, and it was all right with me if it gave him any pleasure, for I liked bananas. I asked the fruiterer how he would like to live in a country where bananas were sixpence for a bunch as big as your head. He gave me a suspicious look and said: "Oh, yes, and gold in the streets too, I fauncy, and awl of yer rides in coaches dressed in silks and satins, tell it to someone else, young person; bananas sixpence a bunch!"

Uncle Ben had a coat and some dresses made for me at a smart dressmaker's on Duke Street, the establishment of a Mrs. Darrelcour. She had never made clothes for such a young lady as myself, but she would do anything, she said, for the doctor's little girl. I've rarely seen a bawdier look than she gave Uncle Ben when she said it. She was rather magnificent, a tall figure in tightly fitted trailing black silk, but too highly coloured. Her massed red-gold hair was held with amber combs, and her cheeks were bluish scarlet; there were little broken purple veins where the skin stretched over her cheek-bones, like the fine silk threads in the paper of a dollar bill. It was a drinker's skin. I soon learned that something was going on there with Uncle Ben, but it was not directly with her.

There was a tall willow wand of a girl, as lovely as a branch of apple blossoms, who passed as Mrs. Darrelcour's niece. She acted sometimes as model and sometimes as vendeuse. She might have been a young duchess so long as she kept her mouth shut; but when she began to talk and show her teeth, she was as common as dirt, and her beauty, for me, was gone. She was one of those unexplainables, one of those slum beauties, a throwback, a flower from the dung-heap; as fresh and lovely as the most cultivated bloom. It was *she* that Mrs. Darrelcour meant to be the doctor's little girl; and the doctor meant me to know about that little girl and tell about it at home. She sidled in and out of the room while the fitter was busy with me, and one day Uncle Ben took her out to tea with us. She had changed from her shop dress of long black silk to a pretty outfit with a beaver jacket and cap, and she looked so pretty I told her so.

"Aow," she said, and it was a pity she smiled and showed her too short teeth and too long gums, "I couldn't afford such pretties meself, Madam had me wear it out to tea, to give the establishment a good name."

"What do you say we buy it for her?" Uncle Ben said to me, and I was slightly nauseated to be included in the transaction by his use of the word "we." I think he was, too. He was used to something better than that girl, but it was helping to divert his mind. The girl was enjoying herself; he had ordered too many crumpets and buns and cakes, and a high dish of sweets. Her eyes nearly popped out of her head, poor thing. She couldn't have been more than eighteen, and treats in that life must have been rare. We could hardly tear her away from the table when it was time to go, and I think that made him like her far more than her good looks.

My new things came home and, as I expected, neither Mama nor Nana liked them. Mama said they were a woman's clothes on a small scale, not a little girl's at all, although she had to admit they were beautifully made. I never told them a word about Mrs. Darrelcour and the lovely girl.

Living in lodgings was a new form for us, pleasant enough and with no domestic cares. The meals were cooked downstairs by Mrs. Jukes in her kitchen, and served upstairs in our sitting-room. She was a terrible cook. The promise of that first wonderful tea was never fulfilled by anything else but tea. Mrs. Jukes could take a duck, and by the special magic of English cookery she could rob it of every bit of its flavour and succulence. Vegetables all added up to cabbage. Mama asked if she might go downstairs to show her the American way to roast a leg of lamb. The kitchen was in the bowels of the earth, under the sidewalk. Mrs. Jukes was resentful, taking a proper pride in the British tradition of the roasting of meat, and one visit to the kitchen was enough for Mama. She didn't like what she saw, and the beef and lamb continued to come up shrouded in beige gravy.

Daddy was having a delightful time. He, too, loved the style, he loved to wear his cutaway every afternoon and his full-dress suit every night. There were late parties at wonderful houses. Wilde and Whistler had established the æsthetic cult, and society mingled with the arts. Mama went occasionally but more often stayed at home. She may have been bored with those parties, she may have felt not up to them, or more likely she knew that Daddy would have a better time alone. That was the way she designed her life. Whatever the reason, it was wonderful for me to have her home. I dreaded the evening loneliness; that awful quiet when I knew a life was being lived all around me, and only I was alone. It was a child's sadness that I felt, full of hope that some day I would grow to live in the adult world of work and parties, and freedom. Those quiet evenings when we were alone she sewed or read. I watched her movements as she pulled her needle in and out, or turned the pages of her book. There was little sound, only the coals settling in the grate, horses' hoofs, and wheels muffled by the curtains, and Mama's soft sighs with her habit of twice catching the breath in her throat. I was watching time go by for my real life to begin.

Uncle Ben was amusing himself in his way, an unpleasant way, I thought, if it included Mrs. Darrelcour and her niece; and Nana had met a gentleman at a party who seemed to be filling up her time. When Nana and the gentleman went off to Paris it made Mama sick. She grieved that Nana could do this foolish headstrong thing, breaking down all that Mama had tried to build up for her these past months and giving no thought to the grief it was causing. She had other worries. At the same time Daddy had to take a big cut in salary, and it was not long before the theatre closed down entirely. I began to get sick and pale from certain of my own terrors.

There was raging in London at that time a series of murders, gory and all alike, the work of a maniac or degenerate. The murders were not confined to one neighbourhood or one class, but broke out in all parts of London. The murderer was the original Jack the Ripper, named for his practice of tearing the knife across his victim's throat. His name alone was enough to strike terror into the heart of a child. He lived with me. I could forget him sometimes during the day, but at night he was in everything. When I had gone to bed, and the window was opened and the light was out and the door closed, I was hurled into a world of mortal terror. I did not know which was less awful, to sit up straight with my knees drawn up under my chin, to see him in the folds of the curtains, to watch for him creeping from behind the sofa, the chairs, or raising his dreadful head from the little black iron bin that held the coals and could not possibly hold a man, or to pull the bedclothes over my head and imagine him everywhere. I dared not fall asleep for fear of his hand on my throat. People collapse from much less terror, and it is a wonder I did not get sicker than I was; stranger still, I never told. I must have been fascinated by the intensity of my terror, for my imagination was enormously stimulated. I stayed awake until daylight, then all the frightful objects in the room were once more plain tables, chairs, or piles of my own clothing. With the light, I would have a couple of hours of heavy relaxed sleep, until the housemaid came in to close the windows and make up the fire. The rattle of the coals in the scuttle was music, so were the early morning sounds of horses' hoofs and the wheels of the milk carts on the cobblestones. Occasionally on those horrid nights the stillness was broken by the sound of a cab, a comforting link between me and the world, for one who rode in a carriage was a gentleman; it was unthinkable that Jack the Ripper could do anything but prowl and skulk in the shadows.

I was nervous and edgy from that secret life. I was afraid that Mama would ask me what was wrong, and I did not want to tell her. Then Nana came back from Paris and there was trouble. She brought far too many things with her, some of them of too much value to explain away. The prettiest of all was a watch that I would have given my soul to own. It was a small sphere of diamonds, with a flattened end that held the face of the watch, no bigger than the nail of my little finger. It was suspended from a bar of diamonds and she wore it pinned to her waist. It was so pretty, so perfect, so marked, that it was the first thing Uncle Ben noticed. There was an awful row about it.

I heard his voice growling like thunder behind the doors of the sitting-room. I was out on the landing with Mama; she hesitated at the door, then went in. She soon came out looking frightened, then Nana came sweeping out in a rage. She was talking very loud and Mama tried to quiet her. Uncle Ben followed; his red beard flamed with anger, and the snarling look on his face was disgusting. Mama was crying and holding on to my shoulder. The core of all the trouble was bobbing up and down on Nana's bodice, the diamonds flickering with her excitement. He let loose with his tongue, calling her names and shouting that she had ruined him, he would soon have no patients left, all the doctors were jeering at him, and he would not be dragged in the mud by her.

"I'm finished," he screamed, "done with the lot of you, whores and rotten actors and their children!"

That was too much; I ran at him, I beat him, I beat him like a crazy child, his body was like a rock to my fists, under his respectable black broadcloth. I beat his back and his sides and ran around in front and bucked my head into his stomach. I yanked at his thick gold watch-chain until it tore away the buttonhole in his vest. I jumped on his perfect shoes with both my feet and scraped my heels on them to spoil the shine. I knew how particular he was about his shoes. I might as well have beaten the Rock of Gibraltar.

Mrs. Jukes came puffing up like a locomotive from her kitchen. Seeing my rage, she thought I was the cause of the fracas.

"What, what's this, on the second floor, what's going on on the drawin'-room floor, why, why, the best floor in the 'ouse, I never 'eard, and on the drawin'-room landin', I wouldn't expect such a noise from my basement, I'm glad the third floor is on its 'oliday, why, a young miss from America rampin' up and down and round her family!"

It made Uncle Ben notice me. He grabbed my arms and shook me until my teeth rattled like castanets. He shook the breath out of me until I was blue, and retching noises came from my throat. I was a convenient small object for his rage, right at his hand, and it is a wonder he did me no lasting injury. I saw Nana's face, and it was a white mask of fright. It took Nana and Mama combined to get me away from him. I was still purple in the face when Mama took me to my room, and when I got my breath I yelled and was sick. Mrs. Jukes came up with a cup of hot milk for me, she said it would be soothing, but it only made me vomit again. Worst of all was my remorse. I thought that if I had kept my temper I might have made things right between them. I could have pointed out that it was silly to fight over that little watch, when he was such a great doctor and she so lovely.

He left us that day, but I never forgot him. When we were back in New York I watched for him in the streets, I looked in the windows of every passing carriage, hoping to see that powerful head and flaming beard. I wanted to set myself right; I never found him. He was the first piece gone from a world I thought would never change.

Our foreign tour was over, the company was prepared to leave for home, when a piece of luck turned up for Daddy. He was offered a part with an English company, something unheard of then. It was only to play a comedy American part, but it allowed us to stay for a time, anyway, and our star generously deposited our passage money home with the steamship company. And he had another piece of luck, more romantic than remunerative. A certain Royal Personage came to the parties at the Garrick Club, heard Daddy, was enchanted with his voice, and commanded a few speaking lessons; it was a princely favour, and there was some remuneration, although not so much as might have been expected considering the reputation for lavishness that the Prince enjoyed. The two things helped to set Daddy up a lot. The play ran for two months; by that time the gutturals were almost removed from the royal throat, and we found the time had come to go back home to America.

When Uncle Ben walked out, he did not leave a penny for Nana. Maybe he thought her companion on the Paris trip would look after her, he may not have thought about anything at all except his own anger, or he may have been glad that she found herself stranded. But the Paris gentleman had vanished from the scene, and Nana had settled down into an imitation of domesticity.

She was extra sweet to all of us. She changed her habits, she took the baby out in her pram in the mornings while Dena was washing and mending, instead of breakfasting in bed and reading for two or three hours. I think she never read a book in her life, but she loved the papers. Aunt Mamie sent her the *New York Herald* from home, and her favourite reading, *Town Topics*. She never missed an issue of it, and read every word. It was a splendid source of information about her gentlemen friends, and about their wives whom she only met in print. She took a long time dressing, not that she fixed up much, but she liked to soak in the tub and brush her hair until all the coppery lights shone out; and she liked to try on several dresses before deciding, for she claimed that the way she felt made a lot of difference to the way she looked in certain things. She used no rouge, but plenty of powder, and the faintest touch of colour to her lips; and that wonderful twist she gave her hair, setting it in loose waves, and fixing it with shell pins.

She left off all her jewelry except the diamond watch, and wore black dresses. But the plainest of her clothes were pretty smart, and had the rustle of silk beneath. Mama said: "Ray, you look sort of like a widow, is that how you feel?" and Nana said: "Sort of," and gave her slanting smile. She had another smile, broad, dazzling, and jolly, with a dimple in her cheek.

She went out one evening with a gentleman who sent a brougham for her. She wore one of her long swishing lace dresses, her feather boa, a turban of spangles, and her diamonds. She said she had to sell some of her jewelry, she had not a penny, and this was a business engagement. We opened the window to watch her go, Mama called down: "Careful now, girl." She had one foot on the carriage step, she blew us a kiss from her fingers, and all her gaiety seemed to have come back.

Next day she told us her friend had arranged to sell one of her rings. It was a large pink pearl, set in a band of rubies that circled her finger, and it must have been valuable, for she got a pocketful of money. She told Mama her friend had arranged to sell it to a lord who wanted something unique to give his girl, and the girl's name was Totty Coughdrop, so help me, and if we did not believe it we could go any night to the Empire and see her, dressed in long clothes—a baby act with a little cap tied under her chin—and she was knocking the army, the navy, and the House of Lords into a cocked hat.

We all went shopping. We bought presents to take home and some strictly British clothes for ourselves. I got a blue tweed reefer with brass buttons, and a sailor with "Victoria" printed in gold on the hat band. Mama and Nana bought the first genuine shirtwaists on the market. We had gone down to Bond Street to have a look, not expecting to buy. They saw the things in a window, marked "New, Exclusive." The waists were made just like a man's shirt—stiff bosom, with studs, a starched standing wing collar, and stiff cuffs. They were expensive, but as Nana pointed out, they were the only things seen so far in London that would mark them as foreign travellers when they got home. They bought bow ties, cuff-links, and, to top them off, each one bought a straw boater. I could not bear those shirtwaists, but they were smart. With the presents for everybody at home, those waists ate up the pink pearl and Nana had to sell her big sapphire and diamond ring.

Mama and Nana were both glad to be going home. Not Daddy and I. I had not realized the strength of my attachment to London until those last days of leave-taking. I loved the well-ordered beauty and the sound of people talking. I loved antiquity, and for the first time I realized a living past. I saw stones that had been touched by Queen Elizabeth's feet, and she became a living woman, not only the picture in my book of a bloodless dressed-up creature, a mass of wired gauze and brocade and lace and crusted jewels. I saw the Tower of London, and Walter Raleigh became a living, breathing, tasting man, uttering his poetry, gallant and loyal, instead of a stale story about a cloak, a queen, and a mud puddle. Daddy showed me a mirror that had held a thousand reflections of Siddons, I tried to see her face there instead of mine, and I saw the huge Gainsborough hat, the fine-drawn features, the swan throat circled with black ribbon, I heard the glorious voice, saw it pulsing her throat, and realized the glorious creature.

All of London was made of things I liked, I forgot the fogs and the rains, the murders and the underdone legs of mutton. I thought of the Palace Guards changing, of Queen Victoria riding out in her carriage and bowing each side, the feather tips bobbing on her bonnet above her plump face. The delicious teas, with wonderful people in beautiful rooms, and the iron key with which I let myself into Torrington Square. That made me feel part owner of London. I gave my photograph to Mrs. Jukes, hoping that she would give me hers in return. The only one she had was taken with Jukes on their wedding trip, it was in a peacock-blue plush frame in her room, and she could not very well give me that; but she gave me a bookmark of purple ribbon with a cross stamped in gold on one end, to keep, she said, in my prayer book. The gold cross was almost rubbed away with her fingering, and it was more like her than her picture. I went into the square and touched the bushes and the railing, I took a twig and a tuft of grass and put them in my purse so I would always have a piece of England with me.

Our hour came, and we left in two four-wheelers and a hansom. Mama and Dena and the baby were in one four-wheeler with the luggage, a gentleman called for Nana and took her in another, and Daddy and I rode in the hansom. He was disappointed and hurt, he hoped up to the last minute that something would turn up to keep him there; but here he was saddled with five women of assorted sizes, going back to America; no more smart parties, no more Garrick Club, no more London elegance. I felt as badly as he did, and I reached for his hand.

"We'll come back again, dear," I said, and I held his hand up to my face and kissed it. He did not answer, his mouth was set in a hard line of disappointment.

There are things that never change. Some of the sounds and sights I know have gone, the rattle of wheels on the city streets, the clump of horses' hoofs and the sounds from the blacksmith shops; the look of long streets and avenues of low houses, of ladies holding up their skirts as they walked, and gentlemen in high hats and frock coats.

But on the way to Liverpool on the train, I watched the changeless sight of trees against the sky; big trunks and strong limbs flowing out with grace, and the etched lacy twigs. The sky was a cold silver, and as the afternoon deepened, it changed to lemon yellow, then to a dark tragic pink at the horizon. Breughel saw such trees, so did Dürer, and the masters of Italy painted them against skies of gold leaf; Vincent saw them in his great delirium, and so will people still unborn.

Daddy sat across from me, holding the baby in his arms. Her head rolled on his shoulder with the motion of the train, her big eyes opened and closed, glazed with sleep. Mama and Nana were talking together quietly, their affection always lovely, and Dena gloomy, was rolled in a rug in the corner of the railway carriage. Daddy and I had the end seats by the window. It was good-bye for ever for us, I thought, in spite of my words in the cab, for where would we ever get enough money to travel so far again? I watched his face, and the hardness around his mouth softened, he looked down at the baby, then at me, he pointed to her little head rolling around, he imitated it, opening and closing his eyes like hers, both keeping time to the rolling wheels.

"Going home," he formed the words with his lips, making no sound to disturb her. It made me cry, then I slept.

It was the end of March and we had a terrible crossing; but the day before we landed, the sea was a sheet of glorious innocent blue. I felt handsome as the day itself, washed clean inside by my many days of seasickness, and I went up on deck to watch for the first sight of land. An old gentleman was standing by the rail, and he lent me a look out of his field glass. We watched all day, and late in the afternoon he shouted: "Here it is!" I looked through the glass; there was a long line of grey more like cloud than land. I expected to see the stern and rock-bound coast of poetry, with sad branches of pine sweeping the water, a white church spire, and some place a roast turkey. I gave the glass back to the old gentleman; his lips were trembling, his eyes were bright with tears, and his bony fingers were opening his overcoat. From the inner pocket he took out a small American flag. It was a beautiful thing, and he must have carried it a long time, for the folds were deep in the silk like a well-ironed pocket handkerchief. He gave it to me to wave, and I forgot the piece of England I had taken from Torrington Square. I was ready to give my life for my country.

Eight

Aunt Mamie's house was full, all but one room that she had kept for Dena and the baby. The rest of us went to the Barrett House on Broadway and Forty-third Street. It was a lovely hotel with rows of push buttons in the rooms and rows of bellboys on benches in the lobby. Ring once for bellboy, twice for chambermaid, three times for waiter, and four times for ice water. You don't hear that sound any more either, ice water clinking in a thick china pitcher coming down the hall in a hotel.

After we had some dinner, Daddy went out to have a look at the Rialto and to find some of his old crowd.

"I know what that means," said Nana, and she lifted an imaginary glass and poured an imaginary drink of whisky down her throat, wiping the imaginary drippings from her mouth with the back of her hand. Daddy thumbed his nose at her and jabbed an imaginary needle into his forearm, making a hissing noise

107

with his mouth. She gave him a smack on his cheek, he gave her a smack on her behind, then they gave each other a loud kiss, and he left, his hat tilted to one side.

I was put to bed in Nana's room just for one night until we could settle in properly. I tried not to sleep, I wanted every minute to realize fully that I was home in New York, but I must have slept, for I awoke hearing the sound of voices from the next room. I opened the door between. There was a crowd, Mama and Nana in their wrappers, Daddy had half a dozen of his friends, their faces shining and flushed, and there was a lot of food and drink. Beer bottles and glasses were on the washstand, and Daddy had some boxes of fried oysters in his hand. I had forgotten about fried oysters. Daddy used to buy them at a place called Mock's on Forty-second Street near Sixth Avenue and bring them home. They were put up eight oysters to the portion in a pasteboard box with four flaps on the top and a handle. A wilted lettuce leaf was at the bottom and on top was a sour coppery pickle that nearly took the skin off your tongue, but it was good. The oysters had a crunchy taste and a fried smell that was like home and Broadway, then you took a drink of ice water afterwards, and there was never anything in the world just like it.

Nobody noticed me at first when I slid into the room and into Mama's bed. Everybody had a glass in hand, even Nana, who rarely drank, but somebody had brought in a bottle of rye, which was the only thing I ever saw her take except champagne. She was standing by the window with a man, an old friend of Daddy's. He was not an actor, he was a press agent and manager for Buffalo Bill and had given me many a ticket for the Wild West Show. He was flashy, common, handsome, generous, and full of love. It showed in the sweep of his black hair, his curling moustache, his light-coloured clothes, and the scarf pin, which was a gold head of Buffalo Bill with a ten-gallon hat of chip diamonds, and his cuff-buttons were made of ten-dollar gold pieces. He was trying to kiss Nana, pulling at the lace cascade in the front of her wrapper, nosing into it like a baby. She was pushing him away with little shoves, but she liked it, it was almost impossible for her to resist an amorous man. I saw her eyes half close, she took his head gently in her hands, for a moment I thought she would take his face to her and kiss it; then there was a change, she was remembering something, she pushed him away and turned around to the rest of the room. I saw her take a lot of small drinks of whisky. It was not the homecoming she wanted, for nobody special met her at the dock but Uncle Ben's dark brother. It was noisy. Bottles and glasses clattered on the marble top of the washstand, and they drank themselves into the singing stage. They all had their arms around one another, and the wonderful humming singing sound went round my head like a wreath and sent me to sleep against my will. The first thing I knew, I was watching the wind blow the lace curtains in at the window, and the sun brilliantly spotting the flowered carpet. It was home weather, March was going out like a lamb, with warm sun and cool winds, deep blue sky and sailing clouds.

Nana was asleep in the other bed, slightly snoring; one hand was dangling down, every finger covered with rings. She must have put them all on to show the boys the night before, and her diamond watch was pinned to her nightgown. Mama was standing looking at both of us. Her big eyes looked sad and her honey-coloured skin was tinted with green. She certainly was not used to drink. We had breakfast upstairs in our rooms just for once, they could not face any dining-room odours that morning.

There was barely enough cash among them to pay the waiter his tip. Last night's party had cleaned them out, and the headachy gloom of that breakfast was made thicker by discussions of ways and means. Daddy said there wasn't going to be a legitimate show on Broadway that summer, but with his voice he might be able to get into a revue, although it would do him no good professionally, still if it was good enough for Lillian Russell he guessed he could trail along and draw a salary. Nana said she guessed she would get a little something from that—and she pointed to me and spelled out the word she called him in sign language, not knowing it was my favourite means of communication with my friend Jesse.

Then they looked at Mama.

"Now don't all jump on me," she said, "I've got an idea. It's no use trying to save a dollar when no dollars come in to save. Anyway, I'm sick and tired of economizing, it ruins more people than extravagance ever did. I've thought about this all the way over on the steamer and my mind's made up. I'm going to rent a house and take enough boarders to pay our living, and you two," she was laughing now, and she leaned her head over to Daddy till her cheek touched his, "you can furnish the fancy work and the trimmings."

"Becky darling," said Nana, and she spread out her fingers on the table, jiggling them so the diamonds twinkled, "if Mamie can do it, you can and we'll all work together."

"If we can make it as pretty as Cousin Julia's beautiful room, it will be a hit," I said, and Daddy said there was an idea in that, and Mama said for God's sake would I finish my oatmeal, and then would I put on my hat and coat and run over to see how the baby was and kiss her good-morning for all of us.

I expected to see changes in the city because I had been in Europe; but the neighbourhood was just the same. The drug store was still on one corner, the grocer, my beloved Mr. Carstens, was on another, the Salvation Army was still in the wooden shack on the corner of Forty-fifth Street and Broadway. A girl was standing out in front, playing on a cornet, low, because it was morning, and the blue light of faith in her eyes pierced the shadow of her straw bonnet. A young man in eyeglasses was beating a drum harnessed to his chest, and they were singing about salvation in muted ecstasy. At night they made more noise, when more people were around to be saved. Dick the newsdealer was on the other corner, he kept store in a wooden lean-to that was built against the brick wall of the last house on the street.

Dick's was a wonderful place to spend money; I could afford anything in his stock; he had slates, slate pencils and lead pencils, book straps, pinwheel papers, and decalcomanias, paper pads from a penny up, blank books, rubber balls and jackstones, valentines in season both comic and lacy, and all sorts of foul penny candy. There were bright pink and green sugar buttons stuck on paper ribbon; nigger babies five for a cent; shoestrings made of rubbery licorice paste, nigger heels made of coconut and molasses, and sandy chocolate creams. He kept all the magazines, which he let me look at so long as I did not rumple the pages and spoil the sale. The first adult stories I ever read came from Dick's stand.

There was a magazine called the *Black Cat,* and for a while my life was lived only from one number to the next. The stories were macabre, patterned after Poe's tales. The magazine was no larger than a pamphlet, and though I have forgotten the stories, I remember the cover. It had a cat's head in black on a scarlet ground, with a white cartouche that held the titles in black. Most of its fascination for me was due to my horror of cats. They were the most dreadful creatures on earth, worse to my soul than the snake. In my wakeful hours I had fantasies, I had them walking on my back, crawling around my neck, I felt the woozy pads of their feet on my face, or a cat biting through the palms of each of my extended hands. When the horror was too great, I managed to drag myself out of it. But the real cat was more horrible than fantasy, for it could not be escaped. I cannot recall ever having touched a cat, but from ages back I knew the feel of its loose furry skin sliding over little bones, and the piercing disgust of needle-sharp teeth.

I found my friend Jesse sitting on the stoop of Aunt Mamie's house. I thought he would be crazy to see me, but no, he was sorting out cigarette pictures of baseball players and barely said hello. He showed me some of his favourites and told me about scores, and I said they did not have baseball in England and he said it was a foolish country and you'd never catch him going there. "But Jesse," and I could not speak, and I saw the scarlet tunics and the great black busbies of the Palace Guard changing, the tommies with little caps and swagger sticks, the bobbies with their helmets held by straps below their lower lips, the flowering window boxes in the houses around Torrington Square, the Queen's carriage, long and graceful, with four horses and four men, the swans and ducks in Regent's Park eating my bread crumbs, the lumbering buses where you sat on top and saw everything, and the little page in red cloth and brass buttons, saying my name into Cousin Julia's room. The ocean had come between Jesse and me.

Nine

We rented a house on Forty-fifth Street directly in back of Aunt Mamie's. Uncle Sol had the wooden fences taken down, and we had a lovely long garden. I had come back to the hotel that first morning sad and hurt because I had not been able to take up with Jesse just where I had left off when we went away. They were all still sitting around the breakfast dishes, and Uncle Ben's brother Louis was there. He was short, square, and stout, he had hair and eyebrows as black as his brother's were red, his face was as red as his brother's was white, and the black undertone of his shaven beard gave his face a purple and apoplectic cast that always frightened me. He was a shrewd man, and had made a fortune in real estate. With all his fleshy look, and sharp practices, he had a passion for the beautiful that I have rarely seen equalled. He was no æsthete, no fade-away colours and stained-glass attitudes for him, but good solid expensive beauty that hit you in the eye. His house, his clothes, his horses and carriages, and his ladies were all that money could buy—even more, for added to his buying powers was the strong will to find and get the thing that would satisfy his certain taste. The minute I came in I knew he was there, for he had a rich smell about him, it was the smell of the dye of his expensive broadcloth, and the rich tightly curled astrakhan of his cap and coat collar, and the remarkable clean smell of his white linen. He, too, was in love with Nana.

She was extra nice to him that morning, she wanted him to be on her side, although I am sure that Uncle Ben had told him enough and he was no fool. She was worried too about Tom Watson. Twenty-four hours is a long time to wait for a message from a man you love, who lives only around the corner. Nevertheless, she was turning on the lights for Louis, leaning close and tracing around his ear with her delicate forefinger, while she told him about Mama's idea.

"You give me a fine piece of fish every Friday, a good piece of halibut with parsley butter sauce for lunch, and the house is yours," he said, going over to Mama and putting his hand on hers.

"If she'd like it," and he looked at Nana, "I'd pave the street with gold for her."

We had Billy Schwartz to move us in, Billy had

116

moved our family and friends since time began. Daddy
said he moved Washington across the Delaware only
the news was suppressed because of prejudice. Billy
had four men working for him. They were square
tough lumpy men, made apparently of iron, their necks
were as red as raw beef, they had black dirt ground
into every pore, and they stank of that combination of
sweat and whisky that is peculiar to moving men. I
wondered if any of them were married, and if so how
their wives were able to stand them in bed. They were
all of one piece, with their striped ticking shirts and
overalls, and it seemed impossible to me that once they
took them off they could ever put on such filthy garments again.

I stood on the stoop with Billy, trying to identify
each piece of furniture as it came in under the cover-
ings of those dingy old quilts that must have been new
once, even as the moving men's clothes must have been
new, and the moving men must have been babies. The
first load was in, the horses were getting a drink out of
their canvas nose-bags, and Nana was giving the men
a good half-tumbler apiece of whisky. The way they
drank it down made my eyes water. Nana said to Billy
she guessed their mothers were copper boilers.

Billy laughed at her from the inside out. The toothpick that he always had stuck in his lower side teeth

kept his mouth from moving much, but the rolls of fat on his stomach rippled under his shiny old suit and shook the elk's tooth on the end of his watch-chain. He gave Nana one of those looks that she got from every man who ever saw her, no matter what his station in life. She made every man feel wonderful, she made them feel perfectly natural, they never need be anything with her but what they really were. A moving man was all right with her, so was a banker, so was Jake, the fishman, and so were the actors and artists that Daddy knew.

It was a sunny day, so Billy and I waited on the stoop while the truck went back to the warehouse for another load. An elegant maroon-coloured van drew up, and half a dozen neat fellows got out. They had on maroon-coloured pants and flannel jumpers to match, with a gold S embroidered on their collars. It was our piano, which had been at Steinway's while we were in Europe.

"Look at them, Billy," I said, "that's the way I'd have them if I was in the moving business. One, two, three, out comes the piano and up the steps all together, none of your—"

"You would, would you, smarty? Let me tell you that's a easy life, pianners, pianners, pianners all day from morning to night, you don't have to fit a bureau into a sideboard, or the dining-table into a bookcase, or put the wardrobe into the icebox, you don't have to keep running back for the ironing board and the clothes basket, maybe filled with pots and pans that the lazy shiksers maybe hid behind the kitchen door just to make you sore after the ropes has been tied on the last load and it's getting dark; maybe you'd give 'em Irish crochet borders to their handkerchiefs, or maybe you'd know how to fix it so their noses didn't run, maybe you know where there's a bunch of boys that never had a snotty nose, maybe those boys you'd get for that business of yours don't even sweat under their arms nor nowheres else."

I had no answer to that, so I told him maybe there was a lot I didn't know. It was dark by the time the last load was in. The men had their last round of drinks, Billy hung around hoping to get a small chunk of his bill, but Nana said it had to be postponed until her settlement arrived.

"Anything to please you, Mrs. Greenfield," he said, shifting his toothpick from one side of his mouth to the other, and he gave her a modified version of one of those looks, "only you know I got to pay my boys spot down." He looked more than a little worried, his eyes wandering from her diamond watch to the huge sapphire on her right hand. "Tell you what I'll do, this looks like shaos here, I'll come around tomorrow and help unpack and maybe you can dig up a little something for me." He did come around and looked on, but I never saw him raise a finger ever, except to beckon.

We had a sense in that house of beginning a little further on than where we had left off. Mama felt that she was functioning, as she put it, on the right side of the account. Daddy had certainly acquired prestige from having trod the London boards, although it did not get him any immediate engagements. I felt my own life had opened up, that I knew a lot about things that I had never known before, about the arranging of rooms, and particularly that even if my friend Jesse, for some reason, did not care to hear me talk about London, still London was mine, to live in and love, and to spin into the web of my daydreams.

Nana was flourishing. Money was settled on her; whether it came to her from Uncle Ben or from his brother was open to question, but it was there in a fine rich stream, a stream wide enough to set up a brougham and horse. And Tom Watson was once more a visitor.

Mama engaged an upstairs girl and a downstairs girl, and a beautiful coloured cook named Amelia. She was a lovely low-voiced Negress of an unguessable age. She was not young, for her hair was a woolly white at the temples. She was the best cook that ever lived and I consider it a privilege that she allowed me to stay in her kitchen and learn to cook. She let me work with her side by side. When she made her pastry she gave me a bowl of flour and some shortening for myself and told me to look at her and do exactly what she did.

"Some folks," she said, "tells you never to touch the shortenin' with you fingers, cut it in with a knife they says, but some folks has han's like lumps of lead, they don't have han's like feathers like we got, chile, has they?" And those dark brown hands went into the flour, swiftly and delicately working the shortening between her fingers, until the mass looked like the finest sand on the whitest beach. "Then you scarce touch it," she said, "you scarce roll the pin over it on the pie board, but all the time you has to wish it thin as thin, and yo han's gets it that way."

She always wore black and white calico to work in, a clean dress and apron every day, and on Sundays it was all black cloth, and out of the drawer of her bureau, with her prayer book, she took a pair of gold-rimmed spectacles. They were part of her Sunday costume, as much as her black velvet toque and her white cotton gloves. I don't think she could see much out of those spectacles as she looked down at her prayer book, in fact I think she could not read at all. She had no need of it. She had an instinctive knowledge and a wisdom, which is what the aim of most education should be.

She was married to a tall black young man named James, about a quarter her age, and they adored each other. He was a chef in a gambling house that my cousin Alfy frequented. I liked him myself, only for the fact that she saved all the chicken livers for him and I had none. "Never get none at the club. Steaks, steaks," he said, "nothin' but steaks, minute a gemman gets hungry it's a Delmonico or a porterhouse." James and Amelia felt that a gentleman should have what he wanted when he wanted it, a lady too, it was one of the laws of nature. That, they told me, was one of the things a darky was for. On his day off he made her stay in bed and take a nap, and he cooked chef's dishes for us; glistening nests of spun sugar, filled with ice creams as rich as Lyons velvet, soufflés and croquettes and creamy dishes.

Our house looked very pretty when it was finished. The rooms were cheerful and elegant. Nana had a set of Empire furniture for her room, a present from Tom Watson, including a tall cheval glass. She spent hours before that glass, not at her face, for she used no make-up. She was interested in her total figure, the way her hat topped off her tailored dress, the way the dress fitted, the sweep of the trains on her tea gowns, and the cascades of lace down the fronts. My favourite tea gown of hers was a moss-green faille silk with a pink chiffon front with ruffles. She had the fine second-floor front room, the full width of the house, three windows across. The baby and I had the second-floor back; back rooms were not considered so desirable, but they were really the best.

Mama took over all the housekeeping and Nana settled into her own way of life. Mama's self-appointed task was to try to make things right for all of us, and her devotion to her sister was heroic. Every time Nana dressed, to go out or stay in or just to beautify herself, Mama was there to put the finishing touches and to see that she looked well from all sides, back as well as front.

I never knew whether Tom Watson's neglect of Nana after our arrival from Europe was due to caution or coldness; it is possible that he tried to break with her completely but could not. Now, often in the night after I had gone to bed but not to sleep, I heard his hansom cab stop before our door; I heard the horses' hoofs, the opening of the hansom's apron front, and the wonderful liquid, silvery sound of the harness chains as the horse shook his head. He usually came at night, late, I presume after his more legitimate social engagements were over. Occasionally he came about six in the evening, and dinner was served to them both up in Nana's room. He sent wine from his club by messenger, and Amelia served everything up there with her own hands;

everything special, squabs or fillet of beef or a duckling just large enough for two. Fruit came in from Hick's in a white cardboard box, every peach or pear or nectarine wrapped in cotton.

I hoped each time I would be invited in but it never happened. Amelia slipped a peach or a nectarine under her apron for me and brought it down, or if anything was left over she saved it for my lunch next day. I watched for her as she came from the romantic room, I expected to see some reflection of delight on her face; but it was brown and serene, and her tread was majestic and slow, with a bare suggestion of the Negro shuffle, a tiny scuff of the foot before each step.

The summer in our new house passed in a succession of days that seemed alike as they were passing. Long stretches of time pass that way, day after day in apparent sameness, and the change is seen only in the sum of days over time. It shows like bits of gold, washed up in a prospector's pan. That summer I grew up. I was given responsibilities, I had to see that my sister was washed and dressed in the morning, and our clothes put away in the closet where they belonged. I hated it but I did it, first because Mama asked me to, second because it spoiled the look of our room to have things lying around. That summer I discovered reading.

There was a public library on Forty-second Street

between Broadway and Eighth Avenue. It was a wide building, a broad flight of steps led up to the door, and over the door was cut in stone the word "Enter." I entered, into a beautiful lofty hall. It was painted a terracotta, and on one of the walls was a plaster cast of the Parthenon frieze; on another wall was painted in large letters: "Printing: the art preservative of all arts." Nothing else but simple oak chairs and tables for readers. The effect of the place was intellectual; I did not realize it in that word, but it was that; it came from the fine coloured large spaces of the walls, and the classic Greek figures of the frieze.

The library stacks were not open to use then as they are now. You had to use a card catalogue, give the number of the book you wanted to the librarian who sat behind a half-door in a kind of cage. I managed to get behind the cage into the stacks and choose my own books. I went through the juveniles in a few weeks and started on the adult books. I began neatly with A; my first book was Grace Aguilar's *A Mother's Recompense*. My excitement at being able to read and enjoy a book was immense, and I was drunk with my new-found world. I read all of Thomas Bailey Aldrich, and through a lot of A's to the B's and started with *Cousin Bette*. The ladies in the cage began to worry, the head librarian called on Mama to see what should be done.

She was a remarkable woman with a religious reverence for the printed word. Mama was a remarkable woman too, and she said that if I understood what I was reading it would make no difference, because I must be ready for it, and if I did not understand it, it would make even less difference.

Still, certain things did seep into my mind from my reading. Those novels led me to believe that the function of the female in life was to be an adjunct to the male in some capacity, as either an instrument of pleasure, an inspiration, a wife to look after his household, or a housemaid or a cook. So I sank into a life of fantasy, I was the centre of a world of lace and muslin, jewels and velvet and satin, nights at the opera, boxes of lilies of the valley and roses, balls, intrigue, soft speeches, and the most private of private dinners, and gentlemen, gentlemen, gentlemen. And I began to understand certain things about Nana.

There was no work for the actors in the summer. Only one revue was on, but every morning, rain or shine, Daddy went out, along with all the other actors in New York, to make the rounds of the theatrical offices. Whenever he would have me I went with him. Beginning at noon, they embroidered Broadway with themselves, in large and small groups, livened by brightly dressed ladies. The ladies did not lounge be-

fore the cafés and barrooms, nor at the edge of the sidewalk as the men did, but they made a pretty ribbon of
colour among them. The girls would form the centre
of a cluster, a lively gay chattering laughing crowd, telling stories, throwing names from mouth to mouth,
pieces of gossip handed round like candy. Who was
palling together, what friends had suddenly become
enemies, what girl had been set up in a flat and how
rich the man was, and how she had been thankless to
the girls who had been nice to her when she was poor.

The Broadway sun beat down on them and up again
from the pavements, hot and dusty, and pungent
odours drifted out from the swinging doors of the barrooms. I sniffed lemon peel, and gin and bitters, beer
and damp sawdust, and over it the perfumes of the
girls. No matter how poor, they always had some sweet-
smelling water, and no matter how poor, they always
looked clean, bright, and pretty. There was a sensible
vanity to them; not the vanity of the vain, of the small-
minded or foppish, but a respect and a pride in the instrument of their performance. For the actor's instrument is himself alone. His bones and muscles, flesh
and skin, his eyes and hair and mobile mouth, all these,
animated by his talent, make the creature that moves
you. He uses himself to hold the mirror up to nature.
Remember the next time you pay your money to see

them, that it is not only weakness that makes these men and women powder and paint and make themselves as attractive as possible, and when you wound them, you wound their flesh and blood.

After he came home, Daddy would get out his pencils and sketchbook and draw. He copied pictures. He was working on an engraving of Claremont on the Hudson that he found on the back of a cigar box. It was a mezzotint, done in dots. He sharpened his pencils very sharp, and he copied the picture dot for dot. It took time and patience, and while he drew I drew him, moving around and getting him from every angle. When I was not with him I tried to draw him from memory. Then I tried other things from memory; and after a while my fantasy life linked itself to the motive power that moved my pencil. People, flowers, birds, and scenes came on my drawing paper. They were not very good, but my own. I grew too fond of the marks of my pencil. I liked the quality of the line the lead made when I drew it across the rough surface of the drawing paper. It was the same with handwriting; I did not care so much what I wrote, I liked the light upward soprano stroke of the pen, and the dark shaded downward stroke, the ink almost overflowing the line in its fullness.

The summer passed, and I had to go to school. I

had been dreading it; I should have been sent two years before, but going to England had interfered, and I had a good ground-work with Miss Pinkney in London. It seemed foolish to me to have to go to school, there were so many things to learn and do at home. I wanted to stay in the kitchen and learn more from Amelia about cooking; I wanted to draw all day, and I was learning to sew. Daddy had an engagement at the Madison Square Theatre for the winter season, and I wanted to be with him while he learned his parts. I held the script while he walked around the room saying his lines, correcting him when he slipped a word, and giving him his cues. He had an amazing faculty for learning lines, an almost photographic memory. He learned the words in their order before he had the meat of them in his mind, and as he said them over and over, the meaning would come into his wonderful face. It was like listening to a melody to watch him, or like watching the play of the sun over a windy field.

Time had always stretched out for me, an endless quantity to do with as I pleased. Now time had pounced on me and was feeding me into that smelly school as though I was sausage meat. I was horrified to think that I might turn out to be like one of the hundreds of unattractive children. I was revolted by them, and by the ugly building and bare rooms where I would have to spend so much of my life. The rooms smelled of a combination of spit and slates and stale clothing, and unwashed children. I never entered my classroom without my stomach turning, and I never got used to the smell, no matter what they say about it. My fastidiousness was shocked, I knew nothing about the friends I would make, the joys of competition, and the growth of my own mind under teaching. And I was nobody's darling at school the way I was at home. It seemed to me that the teachers looked upon the children as so many little enemies that had to be conquered. I did not like them and I guess they did not like me; at first anyway, for later on in my school life I grew very fond of some of the teachers. They all had too much to do and were always harassed.

So I turned inward to my secret life. Home took on the colour and beauty of a dream while I was away from it. Nana with her beauty and luxury, with her lovers and wonderful clothes, became a fabulous woman, as though I had created her myself. Nobody in that school would believe any of it about her, nor about the rooms at home, with the candlelight and flowers. I could drone out the multiplication tables to the bored teacher at her desk, with that cloudy dream life above me. It was a dangerous practice and it's surprising that it caused me no more trouble than it did. My mind being so caught in itself, I could only learn subjects that were interesting to me. Those subjects came easy, and I failed in the others. Strangely enough, I was good at arithmetic. Numbers caught my imagination, the infinity of the ten numerals in their endless combination was magic. I spent hours arranging and rearranging the symbols on my slate.

I walked to school every day with a girl who lived across the street from us, a girl by the name of Jean, and I adored her. We were as different from each other as her family and household were different from mine. Our walks to school every morning would have been sheer delight to me if school had not been at the other end; and there was one other unpleasantness, I was always afraid of being late. Lateness, a little seed of an idea in my head, grew to be a big overshadowing plant of worry. I was up and dressed and over calling for Jean long before she sat down at table for her breakfast. I went crazy with nervousness watching her and waiting; at the same time I was fascinated by her slow and elegant movements and by the fact that she did not worry at all about being late. That seemed singularly aristocratic.

For some strange reason, another thing that raised that family to heights of refinement was the fact that they ate bacon without eggs for breakfast. It seemed lordly and high-handed to break up the combination; and they got their cook up in time to make hot muffins for breakfast. At home Nana had her breakfast in bed, any time she woke up, depending on the night before; Daddy came down about noon, trying out his voice up and down the scale as he came down the stairs, and he ate a lot and drank coffee and hot milk out of a bowl, holding it in his hands and wandering around the parlour floor; Mama walked around with a cup of coffee and I had my breakfast at the kitchen table from the cracked thick crockery the servants used. But Jean and her mother and grandmother sat at table, dressed in fancy dressing sacques, her father silent over his newspaper. The grandmother poured coffee from a splendid silver pot, and served the bacon from a silver platter. The slices slithered around on the shiny surface and her old hands trembled, but she caught them eventually. It all took time, and I don't know why I tortured myself waiting, except that Jean was the bright necessity of my life. They never offered me anything to eat or to drink, not even a nibble off the hot muffins that nearly drove me crazy with their crusty smell.

The walk to school was two things, delight in my friend and the harrowing fear of lateness. Before I knew Jean, when I walked alone in the morning, I would sometimes be so early that the emptiness of the school street sent a pain through my middle, thinking it was so late that all the children were already in the building. It was agony walking with her; I tried to leave her but she enchanted me. She had a graceful long stride, never quickening her steps. I tried not to show her my fear, and I used subterfuges to get her to move along, even pretending to linger, so that it would react on her. But she had a cruel aptitude for cutting it so fine that we just made it before the doors closed, with my heart in my throat.

I have never lost that compulsion of time. After a few weeks of those walks to school, I developed an ailment. I awoke in the morning lying on my bed, fully dressed except for my street coat and hat, which were downstairs in the hall closet; I had no remembrance of a single motion of dressing, but I felt pleasantly tired and relaxed, and strangely relieved of tension. Betty discovered me one morning, went running to Mama, and there was a lot of to-do about it. I begged them to let me alone. But Betty came to sleep in my room on a cot, she tucked the covers tight around me at night, and said a Catholic prayer. She assured me that the Mother of God would not let me be late for school, while Betty was there to wake me. She wanted to lock my clothes away in the closet at night, but Mama thought that would be dangerous and she was wise, as always. By spring my somnambulistic dressing was over, but never my worry about being late. That has made me a good scene designer.

Walking home in the afternoon was different, that had home instead of school at the end of it, and I could dawdle and look at things; particularly Brewster's carriage works and the Horse Market.

The Horse Market was at Fifty-first Street and Broadway. The building is now the Winter Garden. Everything focused on the horse, and the money for it and from it. The building had a tanbark ring, spanned by iron girders that held the arching glass roof. The glass was thick and green and never washed, and the light filtering through it was like light under the sea. Motes of dust rising from the ring gave the atmosphere a golden haze, so that anything a bit beyond where one stood had a texture like painting on a canvas. A crowd was there every afternoon. Fashionable ladies and sporting ladies, swells in grey toppers and all kinds of men who had to do with horses, from youths with ambition for jockeydom to men too old for the business who could not stay away from the horses; in tight trousers and chequered vests, horseshoe pins stuck in their Ascot ties, and those warped legs shaped like wishbones that horsy men are either born with or acquire.

Horses were always being tried out in the ring; horses in fragile skeleton sulkies, arched necks, arched forelegs, clods of tanbark flying out from swift hind legs. Or a display of riding; men in fine riding clothes or stablemen in clothes that looked as though they had never been taken off. Or a lady with her groom or her husband or her friend, trying out a prospective buy, in a long flowing habit of cloth, a silk topper or a black bowler on her head, her shiny boot showing a tip beyond her skirt, her right knee holding the pommel, her right hand holding the reins, and her left hand holding the gold-tipped crop. Her round well-fed backside went up and down with the motion of the horse, and I thought how pleasant it must feel, and that some day by hook or crook I must manage to be rich and ride a horse, and know that wonderful sensation of the riding rhythm, my flesh against the saddle leather, my arms and hands following with a churning motion as we went around the ring, horse and woman one.

One night I woke from my sleep screaming; the screams came into my ears and out of my mouth. At the same time fire engines were screaming too, hoofs pounding on the cobblestones and bells clanging. The noise was louder because it was night. I ran downstairs and everyone was on the front stoop in wrappers or half dressed. The screams were unhuman, ear-split-ting; then they were topped by a great clash of shattering glass. The house walls and the stones of the street vibrated with the noise. It was the Horse Market burning, and the horses had been trapped in their stalls. There was no help for them: the tanbark was tinder and the wooden part of the building went up like a match-box. By morning nothing was left of the building but the stone foundations and the iron girders, the same girders that support the roof of the Winter Garden today.

The Brewster carriage works was the next spot of interest. The building took up an entire block front from Forty-seventh to Forty-eighth Street. It was set back a space from the sidewalk, and a flight of steps went up to the entrance over a trench-like areaway. The edge of the sidewalk was protected by an iron rail. On either side of the door were two big windows; in one was a brougham, black and shiny, as though it were carved from jet; the spokes of the wheels were painted yellow and the carriage lamps were silver-plated. In the other window was the most romantic vehicle I ever saw: a sleigh, long, low, and deeply luxurious, a series of melting curves. It was a rich blue, the upholstery in Russia leather to match. The back runners curved way up behind the seat, and were finished with metal standards tipped with tassels of horsehair dyed orange. The front runners curved up beside the dashboard, ending in metal spirals and carrying a string of silver sleigh bells. Thrown across the back of the seat was a robe of red fox. You could feel the icy wind blowing through your hair, nipping your nose and cheeks, the pressure of a hand on yours under the warm comfort of the fur, and you could hear the silvery, jouncing bells.

And down below in the basement was the other world. There was a forge and a furnace and anvils. By kneeling down and pressing my face to the railing, I could see. Men were picked out from the blackness by the light from a few gas jets, but mostly by the flare from the furnace and the light from the red-hot ends of the iron bars they were hammering. It was like a Sunday-school picture of hell, as the picture of conventional heaven was a cloud in space, overcrowded with people standing thick as sardines in a box. The men gleamed with sweat and oil, and the scene had a lurid splendour.

It took a long time before school was anything to me but a distasteful necessity. Teaching was as much of a chore to the teachers, I am sure, as learning was to me. Occasionally a spark of interest appeared in the teacher, but on the whole it was a dreary business all around.

Ten

Nana was in the full flower of her life. She was never better to look at. Hers was the style that was improved by the slight hint of maturity that the thirties was bringing to her. She had a brougham with a dapple-grey horse, her clothes were magnificent, and she sparkled with jewelry; she sparkled, too, with the satisfaction of the functioning of her life. She had what she wanted. Yet it was not enough.

A distant relative of ours came up from the South to take charge of the New York branch of his father's business. He was at our house a great deal, and immediately fell in love with the whole family and with Nana in particular. Cousin Gus was soon as much a part of our household as the parlour furniture or the dining-room table.

It was not a kind fate that brought Cousin Gus to Nana at this time; not kind to him. She was hurt and growing angry, and she did not know how to make

matters any better. And several times when I went into
her room, I saw the gleam of the needle in her hand.
She could not, or would not, meet physical or moral
pain in any other way. He lived in bachelor apart-
ments, not so common then as they are now, and
rather wickedly romantic in idea. Men lived with their
families, or in boarding-houses, or were married; and
a bachelor apartment meant a life of freedom, presumably to receive visits from ladies who would not have
been otherwise received. There was nothing wicked
about Cousin Gus. He was large, well dressed, good as
gold, and ineffectual. He was a fine physical specimen.
I heard that he had been a football star at his university,
and that was that. Some strange illness had deprived
him of the hair on top of his head, and he wore a toupee,
the first I had ever encountered, and, to my mind, an
insuperable barrier to a love-affair.

He was in love with her, so bemused that he walked in
a dream. It never occurred to him to ask her to marry
him. He knew about Tom Watson. All he wanted was
the most humble place in her life, and he had it. I believe
that she would have married him just then, although it
would never have lasted; but she was ready to do anything to impress her lost lover. Whenever she wanted
him he came, and he was dismissed at a moment's
notice, hustled out, and hidden even in the bathroom

when the hansom drove up unexpectedly. I always knew when one of the private dinners was to be, for I was in the kitchen with Amelia every afternoon when I came home from school. The dinners were fewer, and sometimes, when I had seen the sweetbreads or squabs in the icebox, a messenger would come with a huge box of flowers and a note, or the hansom would drive up in the late afternoon and after half an hour or so I heard his strange, majestic limping tread coming down the stairs. It made me feel terrible, for I thought Tom Watson was the most magnificent person I had ever known. Young as I was, there was something in his life that touched mine; not Mama nor Nana nor Daddy knew it, but he and I knew it, from the day we looked at the *Grey Lowery Day* together. More and more in my daytime fantasies I lived a life of close communion with him, a dream life of understanding and conversations about Tanagra figures, paintings, and porcelains; a life of beautiful rooms, beautiful food, and the sounds of his hansom cab.

Theatre business was good, and Daddy had plenty of work. Daly's Theatre, the Lyceum Theatre, Wallack's Theatre were going full force. Charles Hoyt was producing his farces at the Madison Square Theatre. While it was not a repertory company there, still he had pretty much the same cast in each of the plays. In those days an actor was an actor, and he had to be able to act any kind of part; so sometimes Daddy was a beautiful young Texas ranger, full of love and romance, or an old fellow with a yard of whiskers, in a loose Prince Albert coat, full of nefarious schemes. Whatever he played, he was good, and to me a fine actor, although never a genius; and under the characterization he was always his gorgeous self. He was personally one of the most popular actors in New York; the profession came in and out of our house like water through a sieve. Many came again and again, and I don't know how Mama managed to do what she did with the serving of meals. There was always a big dinner at six thirty, and about three or four nights a week a meal was served at midnight. Daddy ate his chief meal after the show. He said it nourished him more to eat after his work was done. Amelia was always up, no matter what time it was, and if there was not plenty of cold meat left over from dinner, she would cook up something special. She hovered around them in the dining-room. "These folks," she said, "has to be pleasured after dey work so hard to pleasure other folks."

Our house was three rooms deep on the first and second floors; a parlour, back parlour, and dining-room on the first floor, and on the second floor a big bedroom the width of the house in front, a smaller one in the middle, where the hall cut it, lit and aired by a shaft, and a full-width bedroom in the back. The baby and I had the back bedroom. I was sent up to bed presumably at nine; never to sleep. Betty put out the gas and raised the window, but as soon as I heard her go all the way downstairs, sure that she was in the basement, I lit the gas again and turned it very low. I had my school lessons and piano lessons and practising to do in the afternoons, but these velvety quiet hours were mine to read. The window had been opened and the furnace register turned off; I put the blanket close up around my neck to keep warm, for I did not think it was fair to get up and close the window. Daddy came in with his latch-key; I heard the front door bang shut, and then the front door bell rang and rang again. I got up and went over to the register and turned it on. My room was directly over the dining-room. Every sound came up the pipes through the grating. I sat shivering, my ear glued to the ironwork, hating to miss a thing. They talked and they laughed and they sang. Even without seeing them, it seemed like a golden time. Those rich theatrical voices rolled out, mounted and mounted up to the second floor. Nights when it was not too cold, I stayed there on the floor until sleep overtook me at my post. When I could not stand the wind from the window, I put on my wrapper, which, for some reason, did not seem a legitimate thing to do, or went to bed. One night it seemed so hilarious I put on my wrapper and crept down the stairs.

They were singing Irish songs; it must have been a sort of party, because the crowd was larger than usual. No one noticed me at first, and I stood at the dining-room door watching. Our copper chafing dish, polished like the sun, was at one end of the table, and Daddy was beginning to make one of his famous Welsh rabbits. He poured in ale from a stone jug, then a lump of butter, and when that began to boil, he put in the cheese cut into little pieces. It had to be just the right kind of cheese, the right age and flavour, and he spent hours going up and down Eighth Avenue sampling at the grocery and delicatessen shops. Then he took a big kitchen spoon and put some dry mustard into it and filled the spoon with Worcestershire sauce, mixed that together well, and put it over the cheese; then a sprinkle of salt and pepper, lowered the blue flame under the dish, and let it cook gently until the cheese was all melted. He stirred it from time to time from the bottom up, so it would not stick or burn; then when it was completely melted, he put in two eggs that had been well beaten, stirred it up like mad, turned out the flame, and there it was, running melted gold, light and stringless, eaten on toast. The smell was indescribable, and by the time it was finished everybody's tongue was hanging out, including my own. I edged my way in, and one of the voices said: "Lady Macbeth, as I live, in red eider-down and no slippers!"

It was S. Miller Grant, and he was known as four-and-twenty grave-diggers, because he had played either the first or the second grave-digger to twenty-four different Hamlets. He was playing in Daddy's company, and it was one of the first parts he ever had that was not in a Shaksperian play. He was forty-five years old, and had begun in England when he was fourteen. He was sitting beside Mama, holding her hand, but when I came into the room he caught hold of me and I sat on the corner of his chair. Mama said: "Now you'll catch cold without your slippers." But she knew I never caught cold, and Daddy said: "Come over here, Lady Macbeth, and help me put the toast on the plates." But I ran first and got my slippers, skimming the stairs up and down.

Cousin Gus was there, standing at the sideboard with Nana, drinking whisky. He was flushed, maybe taking too much, and he had an expression of imbecilic happiness on his face that made me turn my head away. He wore dinner clothes every night, and his stiff bosom always creaked. She wore one of her grand tea gowns, a rose silk, all lace at the front and the sleeves;

her eyes were dreamy, and she was giving him one of her slanting smiles. It was not her best kind of smile, but one of her most disturbing. She had a fork in her hand, poking around in a dish of Uncle Sol's dill pickles. The front door bell rang, and the fork flew out of her hand and clattered onto a plate. But it was only one of the fellows who had gone out to get some more bread and ale.

Amelia came up from the kitchen with piles of toast. I helped to serve, and had a quarter of a piece of toast myself with plenty of the rabbit over it. It seemed to me that everybody was talking loud and a great deal. Then they began to sing. An Irish actor named Boucicault gave us some lovely Irish airs: "Believe me if all those endearing young charms," "Acushla," and so on. An actor named Dixey gave us a song he was singing in a show: "If you see a young man," and so forth; and an actor named Powers sang us a song from *Ermini*. He had not much voice, and what there was sounded hoarse, but he was wonderful. An actor named Power then obliged with Cassius' speech: "That you have wronged me doth appear in this," Daddy filling in the Antony part. Then S. Miller Grant said: "How about the sleep-walking scene from our little Lady Macbeth?" I said I did not know it all yet, but would they like "Full fathom five"? They all laughed, and I told them I was learning Ariel with Daddy, and my favourite line in it so far was: "Enter Ariel, invisible." I said that showed what could be done in the theatre. They all laughed some more, and Daddy lifted me on a chair to speak the verse, and he stood beside me and held my hand, for he said it was far more beautiful if I made no gestures. That was the way he taught me to speak my Shakspere. He said I should feel it in my middle, then in my head, then it would come from my throat in the proper flow.

> Full fathom five thy father lies;
> Of his bones are coral made;
> Those are pearls that were his eyes;
> Nothing of him that doth fade
> But doth suffer a sea change
> Into something rich and strange.
> Sea-nymphs hourly ring his knell:
> Hark! Now I hear them— Ding, dong, bell.

He had taught me how to make the sound echo through the cavities of my head, and the "ding, dong, bell" came through in a great volume. S. Miller had hold of Mama's hand, and I had held her eyes through the verse. Her eyes had grown larger and larger to my vision, until I thought they were changing into something rich and strange. The whole company gave me

146

three cheers, and in the middle of it the front door bell rang again. Nana was still at the sideboard with Cousin Gus. This time she did not pay much attention to the bell until Amelia appeared at the dining-room door. She looked at Nana and jerked her head in the direction of the front door. A blanket of quiet settled down; then S. Miller said even Ariel needed some rest, and he picked me up and carried me upstairs, and all the way we both kept saying: "Ding, dong, bell; ding, dong, bell."

One afternoon I came into the parlour about five o'clock to do my practising, and I found Nana and Cousin Gus and a gentleman having tea together. Amelia was fooling around, fixing things here and there and looking a trifle sour. She should have been down in the kitchen cooking dinner, and Betty should have been serving tea, but there were certain things connected with Nana that she felt were part of her life in the household.

The gentleman and I looked at each other with instant dislike. He was a very handsome man, awfully well dressed, but with not a spark of beauty to him. His name was De Forest, and in the flash of my first look at him I knew his eyes were a taste too close together; and when he gave me his flash of smile, with a perfect row of teeth, I knew there was something wrong about the way his jaw narrowed toward the back. Yet he was considered at that time to be one of the handsomest men in New York society.

De Forest was Cousin Gus's big mistake. Poor Cousin Gus had to go to business; he neglected it shamefully for Nana, but De Forest apparently had no business at all. He was married and had a child, and lived with his wife's family in a fine house on Madison Avenue in the Murray Hill district. He was one of that small regiment of men who managed to live without money, without anything but credit. It was a convention that tailors and haberdashers and liquor dealers never needed to be paid, not by gentlemen anyway. He was always the pink of perfection. He ran to black and white check or pepper-and-salt in the morning, something with stripes in the afternoon, and always spats. How I hated spats!

Cousin Gus introduced us, and De Forest rose and shook hands with me, as though I was a young lady.

"A great pleasure to meet such a charming young lady at tea," he said.

I wanted to make some sort of clever reply to that, a sort of society reply, but I could not, and stood there quite dumb. He presumed I was looking at him with admiration.

"I hate to think what those soft brown eyes are going

148

to do in a few years," he said, still holding my hand, and I felt my hand turning to something unpleasant in his.

"Please, please," said Nana, in rather a fancy voice, "don't put ideas in her head. What with acting and one thing and another, she has a great deal to learn still."

"Mr. Watson wants me to go to art school as soon as I finish regular school," I said. But that was not so at all; I made it up then and there. It is true I used to draw a great deal, and I saw and thought of things in shape and colour. I was a wizard at doing maps at school, and one day when Mr. Watson was at the house I showed him some of the pictures I had drawn, and some drawings of what I considered the ideal of womanly beauty. One of them was a picture of a princess sitting at a window embroidering, and her hair was so long that it went out of the window, curved around the turret wall, and came in at another window. It amused him, and he said at the time that I might be an artist some day. But the idea of going to art school had never occurred to me until the story popped out of my mouth.

Mama did not like De Forest any more than I did. So we both kept out of his way, which was not easy because he was in and out of the house at all hours of the day and night. I even met him one morning going downstairs when I came up from my breakfast in the kitchen. I turned back down the kitchen stairs, but that did no good, he had been there just the same. It worried Mama. She had a lot to worry her, and she was looking ill. Daddy was having a good season that year, but he was drinking, and I am afraid that he did not contribute much of his salary to the household. He had taken to staying out for dinner between matinees and evening performances, or else he brought home a girl called Aggie for dinner, a little thing with a lot of blond curls all over her head, and narrow helpless hands. One day I found Aggie crying in Mama's room, and after that she did not come for dinner again.

Mama should have had a happier life; she should have been married to a different type of man, and although they both loved her, Daddy and Nana should have given more thought to her. They took it as part of nature, like the sun and the rain, that Mama should attend to everything and make no demands other than the flow of affection; but she loved us all too much and that love made her vulnerable. Our household must have been extravagant beyond anybody's means, and I often saw that money frown on her face. The servants never complained, no doubt they were well tipped; but her colour was bad, and when she went up the stairs she went slowly, and she said her bones ached. But she went to market every day, and she sat at the head of the dinner table and carved and served, and managed everything in her beautiful, calm way.

Nana was leading an incredible life. It was a four-ring circus, and lasted twenty-four hours a day. But she had periods of two or three days at a time when she stayed in her room, and nobody but Mama or Amelia came near her; and when her door opened, there was always a strong smell of aromatic spirits. Those days nearly did Mama in. She could hardly bear the strain. One day when things were particularly bad, she sent for Uncle Ben's brother Louis. He stayed with Mama in Nana's room for a long time, then he went out to fetch a doctor. Louis never left the house for two days, until the doctor said she was out of danger. A nurse had come, and I was glad that Mama was relieved of the physical strain. Nana had taken too much that time, and when she was up and out of her room again, she was nervous and could not bear a sound.

De Forest came several times during that spell, and once Amelia smuggled him up into Nana's room. The nurse rustled and crackled in her starched blue and white, and came down and complained to Mama, but Mama said if Nana wanted so badly to see him, maybe it would do her good. For a couple of weeks there were no more midnight suppers, and everything in the house was still. Louis took her out for her first drive. She looked a little bit yellow but wonderful in a tight princess dress of hunter's green broadcloth with a toque hat of cock feathers, and two superb Russian sables tied around her neck. He brought them to her, he said, because she got better for his sake. His face looked more purple to me than ever, and his black eyes more piercing. I liked him, and though there was something extraordinary about his taste, his passion was for the best and most beautiful of everything.

He took her out again a few days afterwards, but did not come into the house with her. I was practising my piano lesson in the parlour when I heard the carriage drive up, so I went to open the door for them, but the coachman had already started up the horses, and Nana was watching the carriage disappear down the block. She was furious, and did not stoop to kiss me when I put up my face to her.

"Where's Beck?" she said, and her voice shook.

"Mama's lying down with one of her headaches. Please, Nana, let her be," I said, trying to think how I could take Mama's place.

But Mama had heard the carriage also and had come out into the hall to see if all was well. All was decidedly not well. I don't know whether they noticed I had followed them up into Nana's room. I heard it. Louis had said to her that things could not go on as they were, and had asked her to marry him. He said he knew she was not in love with him and never could be, but that he was in love with her, and that he was a very rich man and wanted an establishment of his own. She would have the finest house in New York, the finest carriages and the finest horses; that his fortune was big and would increase, and that it would all be hers. He would see to it she had a healthy life, and no more nonsense.

"And then," said Nana, "he laid down the law. He said if I did not marry him and right away at that, he would marry someone else, and I could do without him. You know what that means, Beck," and she put out her right hand, rubbing the tips of her two front fingers against her thumb. "Money. But I never could, oh, never, never in the world."

"Oh, Ray, what a wonderful solution it would be! You could settle down to life, have everything you want, no more of this awful strain." Tears were bright in Mama's eyes. I could see she felt the burden lifting from her shoulders. "He'd make some woman a splendid husband."

"I wouldn't go to bed in the same room with that man every night, not for a million in cold cash." She looked around the room in a sort of helpless anger, and her eye caught mine. "Would you?" she said to me.

"For God's sake, Ray," said Mama, "how can you talk to a child that way?"

Nana came over to where I was standing by the window. She took all my curls in one hand and raised my chin with the other.

"It wasn't a nice thing to say, darling; will you forgive me? Do you love me?" I looked at her; I wished I could tell her how much. "You wouldn't want your Nana to be unhappy, would you?" She let my hair go, although she still held my chin, and she turned to Mama. "She has to know about things some time."

"Mama's got an awful headache," I said, and then Nana was all loving and sweet and warm to her. She took Mama upstairs and made her go to bed, and I went down to the parlour and finished my half-hour of practising.

Louis had been coming to the house ever since we moved in, most often for dinner. He loved fish; he said he could eat it nine days a week. He stopped on Thursdays at the Fulton Market and his coachman brought in a big hamper filled with layers of cracked ice and fish, salmon, flounder, and halibut, and those tiny mackerel as sweet as a nut. Sometimes a hamper just filled with hard-shell crabs. Amelia boiled them with a big handful of sugar in the water. She split them and cracked the claws and served them on platters of shaved ice for a first course at dinner.

Now he came no more. He sent in his cheque to Nana as usual. Part of it was her settlement, but most of it came from him, and the strange part of it was that she had no qualms whatever about taking the money and using it. It was needed, for she had never been more extravagant. Then the stableman told her that the bills for the care of her horse and brougham were no longer to be met, and the coachman came with the same story. The coachman, a young Irish fellow, offered to stay on, but what was the use, she said, if she had no turnout for him to drive?

"Ma'am," he said, "a sweeter lady I never hope to drive, and I will pray to the holy saints to increase your fortunes." He could not bear to leave, and I hated to have him go, for he had that wonderful stable smell about him; it wafted into the room every time he moved. It was a world itself.

There was no doubt that Nana was upset about it. But the real blow fell when Mama got a letter from Louis telling her that he had married, and announcing that he would henceforth send only the sum coming to Nana from her divorce settlement, but if Mama was ever in need of anything for herself or the children, to call on him. The letter ended saying: "You are a good woman, Rebecca; any man who has you for a wife should fall on his knees in thankfulness. I am sorry if any of the burden of my course of action falls on you, and I am afraid it will. I find that I must manufacture my own happiness, and this is the only way."

He had married a great beauty. She belonged to the class of kept women who seemed to hold some golden secret of life. Their pictures were sold in stationery stores among the photographs of such theatre stars as Lillian Russell, Della Fox and Mrs. Kendall, or the matinee idols, Maurice Barrymore, James K. Hackett, Chauncey Olcott. I had all their pictures myself, a good hundred of them, but mine were gifts, many of them inscribed, and my collection was the envy of my school friends. This woman Louis married was far more beautiful than Nana. I never saw her, but Dick got her picture for me and he said she was a rip-roarer. Her eyes looked out from the picture, very clear and with a friendly searching look, a look to make any man tremble. Her smile was sweet, curved and suave, not a slant to it. Her hair was parted and waved down over her ears, and done up in a knot on top of her head, and pinned to the knot was a diamond fleur-de-lis. Her dress fell off her shoulders, and there was a perfect curve from her ear to where the dress began, and her breasts bubbled up over the top of it showing the roundness and the cleft but just escaping the impossible exposure of the nipples. Dick was right.

There was a milliner around on Eighth Avenue and Thirty-ninth Street where Nana took some of her good expensive hats to be copied. She was a London cockney, tall, florid, and black-haired, and she sometimes made hats for me. Her name was Mrs. Elsom. As I grew older it was my habit to go out a lot by myself after school, so on my way up from the library in the afternoons, I often stopped off at Mrs. Elsom's place. I was learning to sew. I took a great interest in how things were cut and put together. I tried to make doll-size copies of Nana's dresses and hats, even her corsets. Mrs. Elsom's place was the first floor of a dingy flat house, and although it was dirty and dusty, it was full of interest and colour. She had a fascinating stock of things, rolls of buckram and swags of wire hanging from the ceiling, boxes and boxes of feathers, plumes and flowers, wire shapes, yards of velvet, and bolts of ribbon. It was a mess, but she always knew what was there and where to find it, and she let me work sometimes choosing combinations for her when she could not make up her mind. She showed me how to sew wire with a special stitch onto the edge of buckram, and she taught me one of the most valuable things I ever learned: how to use a straight edge, and how to use a bias edge, so you got the best out of them.

Other things would appear and disappear from the lowest of her stock shelves: crystal bowls and silver things, trays, pitchers, and magnificent linens. One day there would be a lot, another day nothing, and she herself was not there all the time. She came in and out in a big black velvet hat with feathers and a rhinestone buckle and a long cape. She had a high-yaller girl for a helper who was a wonderful milliner and a slick storyteller. A couple of men came in while the high-yaller was showing me how to fringe out some ribbon.

"You cuts the selvage both sides about a inch, then you take yo sizzer an' starts strokin' it down, like you was strokin' yo feller when his haid feels sore. All the squzzles of stuff falls on the floor, and yo has long silky tresses at the end of the rib'm. Yassir, Miss Els'm's out, she says wen yo calls just to say she' out."

I didn't like those two men who came in. They gave me an unpleasant feeling at the pit of my stomach that did not leave me for a long time. The feeling pierced me when I saw a cut crystal bowl full of stewed fruit on the supper table one Sunday night. I had seen that bowl with its silver rim only two days before. I had seen it come out from under Mrs. Elsom's cape and go on to that lower shelf. A long thin sapphire-blue velvet box had come out of the depths of that cape, too.

I said it was a pretty bowl, and had I ever seen it before, and Nana said that Cousin Gus had given it to her for a present; but I couldn't eat any of the stewed cherries, and I liked them a lot, too. Cousin Gus looked pleased with himself. I think he did not have a great deal of money, and it was a satisfaction for him to find a present that Nana liked. He was always with us Sunday nights. That was the off night for everybody else. Tom Watson and De Forest apparently spent it with their respective families. We always had company, relatives and people who did not belong to the theatre. Our supper table was a sight, literally groaning with food, and everybody helped himself.

One day Daddy said that he loved hard-boiled eggs but hated picnics, so what could he do about it? Nana said that she would fix that for him. She would order a bowlful for Sunday night supper. I looked at him, and I wondered where on earth on our Sunday table they could find room for another dish of anything.

Daddy looked at me and smiled, as though he knew what I was thinking about. I often had that feeling when we looked into each other's eyes in a certain way. I smiled back, for I was thinking how foolish it was to have those big Sunday suppers when we had a big dinner in the middle of the day, and how nice it would be to have one in the middle of the week. "Mr. J. P. Mor-

gan presents his compliments and invites Mr. Frankau
and his daughter Miss Frankau for Sunday evening
supper on Wednesday night, December 22, at 6.30
sharp. R.S.V.P. PS. Bring along your banjo, Mr.
Frankau, and give the house a tune." It would be a
lovely engraved invitation brought by hand.

I found I was thinking a lot about Mrs. Elsom and
her place. I enjoyed the millinery, and liked seeing the
work take form in my hands, and I wanted to know
more about the mystery that I felt. While she was
showing me how to tack on a plume so that it would
keep its place, those two men came in again. She was
evidently bothered; she stammered and turned red and
said couldn't they see she was busy?

"New apprentice?" asked one of them.

"Niece of a customer," she said, "learnin' a bit about
the millinery just for 'er own amusement."

"Handy little thing," he said. "Could get in and out
almost anywheres. Face, too. How would you like to
do a little job for me, angel face?"

"Now, you lay off there, Jeff, and no mistake this
time." And she moved around folding things up and
trying to edge them out. But the one called Jeff stood
over me, looking down with his arms folded, his ugly
eyes beady with excitement.

"I'll wait around and see you home," he said.

I began to feel frightened, and wished I had not been so curious about these people.

"I tell you to lay off there," Mrs. Elsom said. "This young Miss 'as things mapped out for 'er. 'Er aunty's the lady wants the big ring I was tellin' you about."

"Oh," said Jeff, "why don't you get it for her? What you stalling around for?"

" 'Ow many times must I tell you 'e was hout?" and she shouted the last word with a full breath on the *h*. "Shove along now, will you?"

"Ta-ta, angel," he said, "I'll be back again some day when you take another lesson." He did not move for a long time, and I was afraid he was going to touch me, he stood so close. I kept on pulling my needle in and out. It was the only motion in the room, and I felt it acted like a charm to keep him off. A customer opened the door, and the bell tinkled and the situation broke up.

I never went there again, but it was not long before Nana had a new ring. It was a square diamond and a square sapphire set just the two stones together, and I thought it was not pretty at all. Cousin Gus gave her that also, and I knew he could ill afford it.

Eleven

The actor S. Miller Grant used to come in afternoons when he was not busy and read to Mama. She was feeling wretched, and although she did not give up her duties, she rested whenever she could. There was a sofa in the back parlour. It was not a cheerful room, for it opened only onto a shaft, but she said she liked the way the half light made her feel, it was restful. It was always twilight in that room, and ever since the darkening toward evening has given me that sense of worry that I felt about Mama. I was glad he came to keep her company. Daddy and Nana never had time enough, and I could not bear much of it. I had a lot to do afternoons. My lessons were harder, my piano practising took an hour a day; I needed time for things I was making, and I wanted to draw. Aunt Mamie came sometimes, but she and Nana had a pretty bad falling out over something, and the two households did not make so much use of their back-yard communications as they had done before.

I listened to S. Miller Grant reading sometimes. He was reading a story about a man in prison, a man whose only crime had been that he wanted his people to be free. This wonderful man had been put to live in a stone cell; the only light came from a tiny window way up near the top of the wall. He was given the barest amount of food, only enough bread and water to keep him alive, and the jailers allowed him nothing to read, and no writing material, and his free and beautiful spirit was near death; hope had almost left him. Every day that the sun shone it slanted for a moment through the bars of that high window; a little longer, a little less, according to the season. One day when it stayed there longer than he had ever seen it, he noticed a small spot of green growing from a crack in one of the stones of the wall. His heart leapt to that growing thing, so tender, so small, that he feared it would die before another day would give him light enough to see it again. He woke before dawn, straining his eyes, and in the first faint light he saw the thrust of the spearlike leaf. That plant became himself, and his hope of release, and he loved it as a man loves his hope and himself.

He was afraid that the plant would grow too big for its sustaining earth, or that the jailer might see it and tear it down; but it grew, the roots found crevices for

163

their foothold, there was plenty of moisture in the dank stone walls, and when the jailer saw the plant, he merely shrugged his shoulders.

There was a great deal of despair, a great deal of hope in the writing, principally the philosophy of hope; how just one small spark, if nurtured and regarded with the right attitude, will lead to eventual release. I thought it was wonderful. But I never heard the end of the book, for Mama was too sick to hear it herself, and I never had the heart to read it through after the tragic afternoon when Grant looked up from his reading to see Mama ghastly and limp, falling into a faint.

It was a mortal agony. They took her away to a hospital, operated, and brought her back, but she never walked again. Her nurse came home with her, a red-haired woman with a milky skin and a superb physique. She was a Russian, and wore the uniform of the Royal St. Petersburg Hospital, a rich king's blue cotton, with starched white collar and cuffs, and a voluminous apron. The Imperial eagle was embroidered on the pocket of her uniform, and she said she kept it there because she hated it, and when she saw it, it kept her hate alive. I said it looked to me like a broiled chicken embroidered on her pocket, and she said: "Yes, do you laughing Americans always find something ridiculous in the tragic? Everything is a joke here in America.

In Russia they would not let me care for her, this angel, your mother. Here she can lie on her bed and let these hands try to make her body bear its pain in some comfort. There the Cossacks would come. They would rip her mattress with their bayonets, to see if money was hidden there. I have seen my father command his men to such deeds, and he has taken milk from the peasants' children to feed to his pigs to make them fat; and to you, what would those men like my father do to a tender young miss like you? They would make you into a little broiled chicken."

She was brushing Mama's wonderful long hair that soon was to be cut off, because Sister Augusta thought it took away her strength. She braided it into two plaits that hung down on either side of Mama's face, down over the edge of the bed almost to the floor.

"Yes," said Sister Augusta, "some day I go back and you little thing will go with me, and I will show you why it is we do not make jokes. I like jokes too," she said, and her strong stern mouth broke into a wonderful smile. "I would like to sit in a drawing-room with our friends while they make music. Wonderful quartets we had, on Tuesday evenings, and I like to listen to the works of your great Shakspere. Our Russian writers have made some fine translations. He is the greatest writer that ever lived, your Shakspere."

She pronounced it her own way. She said "Shak-es-pe-are-ee." I tried to think what it would sound like in the Russian language.

"Can you say the soliloquy in Russian?"

"Indeed," she said. "Listen."

She stood up straight beside the bed, holding the hairbrush in her hand, and spoke in a great rolling thunder rumble of language. I tried to follow it word by word, but it was only one long sound, no words, and no music, but she liked it. It was all right with me. He was her Shakspere, not mine.

"But that is not any longer a concern for me, poetry and jokes," she said, and her eyes were staring wide with some purpose of her own. "There is too much to mend that is broken, yes, and much to be broken that seems now to be whole!"

She was very strong, and very tender; her head was full of things I wanted to know, a world so foreign to me that I could not even imagine what it was like. Mama was her angel.

Naturally Nana had to make changes in her life. Amelia took over the marketing, but Nana had to take charge of the household. She sat at the head of the table in Mama's place. She did the carving and managed the serving, and I presume she handled the finances. It was good for her, and I think that she was taking less drugs. She was taking care of Mama, as Mama had cared for her for so long. She fixed herself up a work basket, and when Sister Augusta was taking her time off in the afternoon, she patiently did the mending. She did not do it very well, and soon Betty took that over.

De Forest was in the house every day, and they seemed closer than ever, but my own friend Mr. Watson seldom came. I missed him, and one afternoon I went down to his place of business to call on him. I went to talk to him, but when I found myself in his office, sitting across from his writing-table, I could think of nothing to say. He had the basement and the first two floors of a wide brownstone house. It was a splendid place, high-ceilinged and full of rich shadows in the corners. The walls of the room where I sat and talked to him, his own office, were wainscoted breast-high with mahogany and covered above with tooled and gilded leather, and they made a fine background for the few large blue and white vases that were out on view.

"I think it is finer even than your own house," I said, and he nodded and looked around and said: "It's a better scale for me."

I looked around too, and then I met his kind, humorous gaze. We both sat still, and then he said: "Yes, things change. We seem happy for a while, then something steps in and breaks up that feeling. It is hard to believe, isn't it, that what we love will not always be fresh and beautiful and stay just as we would have it?"

Of course I knew he was thinking of Nana, and I knew that he was thinking of Mama, too, for he was being wonderfully kind to her with flowers every day.

"But when things change, it is not the end. That is how we grow."

He took a piece of jade from his pocket and kept looking at it and turning it in his hand.

"You are too young to be wounded, but the bleeding will stop and the scars will be covered. That is as it should be. Scars are honourable and sometimes useful. That is why we must value our present, live in it, for it leaves us; but remember not to love it so that it costs too much to relinquish. Here I am preaching to you like an old country parson. I didn't mean to."

I thought of the present with Mama and a future with her gone. I opened my pocketbook to get my handkerchief, but I had come without one, and that was too much to bear. I did not know until just then how unhappy I was, and I broke down and sobbed into his which he gave me, and I could not help thinking how comforting it was to have a man's fine big clean linen handkerchief to cry into.

"I never meant to do this," I said, "I only came to talk to you. You are so wonderful about pictures, and your porcelains, and you know how things are. Please," and I began to cry again, I couldn't help it, "I want your kind of life."

He stopped turning the jade in his hand, and I tried my best to dry my tears. Then he told me he would do his best to make that life possible for me. "But that life," he said, "comes from nothing I could give you. That life was in you when I came into my dining-room on a rainy afternoon and saw you looking at the *Grey Lowery Day*. Do you remember?"

As if I could forget. Then he gave me the piece of jade he had been carrying in his pocket for more than twenty years. It was a circular piece about three inches across with a round hole in the center, and its surface was covered with Chinese writings. It was worn to a texture almost like skin from the hands that had fondled it for so many centuries. He said that when I felt so sad that I needed help, I should take the piece of jade and look at it a long time and I would find my sadness would fall away and take its place in the proportion of time. He had his secretary, Miss Cullen, come up, and they showed me some of the beautiful things he dealt in—timeless things—and I asked him how he could bear to part with them. And he told me that once a great poet had the same idea. "I wonder what it is the vintner buys one half so precious as the things he sells."

He wanted to send me home in his own cab, but I thought I would rather walk, and when I got home, I went directly to Mama's room. It was almost dark, and I wanted to talk to her and maybe sing. She loved to have me sing to her when it was getting dark. I had a nice voice, and had fantasies about being an opera singer one day. Music was always more to me than mere sound; it was a direct translation of feeling. There were a few songs that meant that dim room of Mama's—a song called "In the Gloaming," and a song of Balfe's about a fair dove, "Oh, fond dove, oh, dove with the white, white breast," and the beautiful hymn "Abide with Me." She liked sort of old songs, too, about pretty Polly Perkins of Abington Square, and she liked "Wait Till the Clouds Roll By, Jenny," and she liked funny ones that I picked up from Daddy—"I'm the Man Who Broke the Bank at Monte Carlo"—which I did with action, as though I had on a high hat and carried a stick, and the Quaker song from *A Trip to Chinatown* —"Reuben, Reuben, I've been thinkin'."

But that day I came home from Tom Watson's feeling better and full of strength. There were two men in her room talking to her. I had never seen them before, and as I came into the room they were about to go. One of them was sitting beside the bed, holding Mama's hand and saying good-bye, and one of them had arisen and was standing near. They were Catholic priests. It was Father Flannery who was sitting on the chair by the bed, and Father Chris O'Reagan who was standing. Father Flannery was a schoolmate of Daddy's. They had gone to school together at Hartford. He was just plain Tommy Flannery in those days. He had entered the priesthood and had just been called to a church up on Amsterdam Avenue, way up in the hundreds; and Father Chris was with him in the church. Father Flannery had seen Daddy's name in the paper and had called at the theatre to find his address, and here they were. Daddy was standing at the head of Mama's bed. He had brought them home, hoping that they could be of some solace to Mama.

They were. And they were solace to me, more than that. Father Flannery came down often to see Mama, and I never missed a visit with him. He knew a great many kinds of things. And when summer came on and Daddy was not playing any more, we got into the habit of dining with him once a week. They had a fine church and a large parish. It was so far uptown that it was almost like the country. They lived well in a big stone rectory beside the church. Four priests lived in the house, Father Flannery, Father Chris, and two younger ones. It was an ugly place; the floors were covered with figured linoleum and the whole idea of linoleum overlaid the house. It smelled that way, and the singularly ugly type of design was repeated in the wallpaper and the hangings. The woodwork was a cheap light oak, varnished and kept very clean. When I first went up there, we drove up in a cab, and all the way I had an idea that the place was going to look like some of the religious paintings of the Renaissance—white plaster walls, carved stone pillars supporting a vaulted ceiling, rich gilded brocade, and somewhere an angel of the Annunciation, and a dove in a shaft of light. I told that to Father Flannery, and he said: "Ah, me daughter, 'tis well to have one's dreams, but 'tis well also to do the best one can up here on Amsterdam Avenue. I know what you have in mind. I lived a year in Italy, and I served in the Cathedral of Siena, and I know the school of painting. The architecture is much finer over there, but the parishioners are more or less the same. They're all poor, none of them can pay their rent, and they have to scrape around to keep soup in the pot; but they all seem able to get their drop to drink of an evening, I'm happy to say."

He never tried to turn me to their religion. I went to church on a Sunday, and I was much impressed, particularly with the way Father Flannery spoke. In real life he still used a slight Irish accent, but in the pulpit it was an elegant intonation, much more like the way the actors spoke. But my heart was not touched by him or the service the way it was when I saw the sun shining on the mall in the park, down the long green alley, or the magnolia trees in blossom by the Sixty-fourth Street entrance; or even all the bright-coloured washing hanging out on the lines and blowing around in the wind, way over west where all the Italians lived.

They had a great deal to eat, very hearty but not nearly so good to taste as our food at home. They always had soup served in a tureen down at Father Chris's end of the table, then a fish served by Father Flannery, then there were always two dishes, a roast of meat, and some poultry, and masses of potatoes, and never a sign of salad.

Nana did not hit it off very well with them. Maybe she was too much occupied with her own affairs, which were enough to keep two women busy. She was trying her best to manage the house, but it was not her line. The tradesmen in the neighbourhood were not being paid, and bills were piling up on the hall table. She tried not to notice them as she passed by.

Jake the fishman came around one afternoon late. I opened the door for him, and he asked politely to see

Nana. I hardly knew him; he was all dressed up in a blue suit and a derby hat, and there were fish scales on his big red hands, but they were scrubbed clean and smelt of yellow soap.

Nana was out driving with De Forest. He had come around with a victoria from the livery stable earlier in the afternoon, and Nana said she would be home after five.

"She's gone out, Jake," I said, "but will you wait for her? Is it anything I can do?"

"Well, not exactly," said Jake. "It's a little matter of business."

He started to take some papers out of his pocket, then thought better of it and put them away again.

"Now, you go ahead with that practising, and I'll just sit in the hall."

"Nana would be angry with me if I let you sit in the hall," I said, delighted that I had an excuse to stop. I hated practising, and I had always wanted to talk to Jake.

He would not leave his hat on the rack, but brought it in and held it in his hand. He was impressed with our parlour. I could see that at first it made him uncomfortable; then I could see him settling into it and enjoying it. He lived over his store in two rooms on the second floor of the house. I had seen his mother putting the pillows and feather beds out on the window sill to air mornings, her head tied up in a handkerchief; or leaning out on her elbows afternoons talking down or across with the neighbours, her sheitel a speck to one side.

"You got it pretty nice here," he said. "Looks like a jewelry store." And he pointed over to the glass cases with the Chinese things. "Have to sell a lot of fish to buy a roomful like this," and he cleared his throat, "and get paid for it, too," he added.

I knew what it was; it was the bill. The bill was there between Jake and me, as though it was a huge white sheet, and it wasn't going to be any fun to talk with him any more, and I couldn't run into his store on a hot afternoon for a piece of ice and maybe get a few clams if he was fixing up a batch on the half-shell for a customer, or a hard-shell crab if he was boiling up a couple of dozen, and one had lost a claw, on the little gas stove back of the store.

It did not seem the right kind of thing to worry about when there were so many other things that were making me miserable. I thought of Mama lying upstairs, never to walk again, and as Jake looked at me he saw something was wrong, and he said: "I shouldn't have said that; forget about it. Only something has come up, something."

"No, you're right; only it's kind of tough just now."

"Forget it. I'll go along and I'll see your aunty another time. Crabs are coming in real good now, Long Island, genuine."

He took up his hat and shook his clothes out ready to go, and I heard the carriage drive up to the door. She might as well know about it, I thought. It was easier this way than if he had gone and I would have to tell her. So I went out into the hall and opened the door for her.

Well, Jake stayed a long time, and Betty came in with the whisky bottle and the pitcher of ice water, and it was nearly dinner time before he left. He told her he had a chance to go into the wholesale, and he was cleaning up the retail business, trying to sell it, and he had to show what a fine profit there was in the store.

"Now, Mrs. Greenfield, books are books, and when somebody takes over this here store of mine, I got to leave those books, and he's got to see just where he is in this neighbourhood. Besides, I got my eye on a house uptown for sale cheap. Flats, Lenox Avenue. I was just saying to the young Miss this is just about the style that suits me."

Nana was gazing at him, and I knew she could finish him off like a sardine on a piece of toast. She was only thinking of how she could do it best without actually giving up. Before he left they had come to an arrangement. He was going to all the other tradesmen, figure up how much she owed, and see what he could do about making a settlement, so much on the dollar. And she was going to help him furnish his new home. She opened one of the cases and gave him a small blue and white vase. "Something to begin with, something to remember me by," and she gave him a smile, full in the face, and he left the house radiant.

De Forest was waiting to leave and in a bad temper. He was no longer trying to make his impression. He had made it, and though they seemed to be crazy about each other, still he was often peevish, sometimes rude.

He was leaning against the wall, his hands in his pockets, his hat on his head, and his attitude was insolent. Jake had no sooner closed the door than De Forest took his right hand out of his pocket, held it out, and said to Nana: "Well?"

Nana looked frightened. She put her finger to her lips and turned her head toward me. She looked magnificent. She had taken off her hat and she was in her best afternoon dress, a bronze-coloured faille silk embroidered with bronze beads along all the edges and great frills of real Val lace at her wrists and down the front. It seemed to me she should have been the happiest woman in the world, but here she was troubled.

"I can't walk home, you know; it's too late," he said.

She took up her purse from the hall table, opened it, and showed him the inside. There was a dollar and some small change. He emptied it into his hand and put the money in his pocket. He put his arm around her waist and started to kiss her, but she shoved him off. He persisted, and as I turned to go upstairs to Mama's room, I saw them holding each other close.

Twelve

If there was any compensation in Mama's illness, it was that she did not see Nana's growing infatuation for De Forest. I was glad that she did not know that Nana was giving him money and owing that money to the tradesmen. Daddy was working, but he was away from home a lot. There were hardly any more late suppers, only once in a while when he came home alone. Very little of his money came home either, and he told Nana he was doing the best he could. "I'm in a fix, Ray, and I wish to God I could get out of it. It's not funny any more."

"Nothing's funny any more," I said, and it was the first word out of me to either of them. They both looked around in astonishment. I guess they did not know I was there. Nobody seemed to think that I had eyes or ears or life at all; nobody but Mama and Tom Watson.

"You're so busy at school, darling," said Nana, "and

with your piano lessons, and all the time I see you drawing."

Daddy took me in his arms and kissed me. It was a sad kiss, and I was sorry for him. I was sorry for myself, too, and when he said he felt dreadful that he was not looking after me better, I could not help crying a little.

"All the girls have their parents come to school and ask about them, all the girls," I said, "but me."

After that Daddy came up to school several times to see our principal, Miss Hoffman, and she was crazy about him. She told him I was her jewel, and would he consent to say a few words in assembly some day when the commissioners were there? My heart was in my mouth, knowing he never got up until noon these days and assembly was nine o'clock, and I would feel dreadful if Miss Hoffman ever found that out. He said yes, he would be glad to, and on the way home I said I would see that he got up in time.

"Time," he said. " 'There is a time in the affairs of men which, taken at the flood, leads on to fortune,' or 'Time hath, my lord, a wallet at his back.' Should I tell them that? Or should I tell them: 'There's a divinity that shapes our ends, rough-hew them how we will'?"

I laughed with him, I always did, and I said I guessed

nobody would notice what was wrong with the quotation.

He did come to assembly and he did speak; he told them that all the world's a stage, and it was up to us poor players to strut about and to see that the stage was clean and, above all, beautiful.

"Try to see everything in a harmony," he said. And I could see that he was telling them to do what he had not been able to do with his own life. "Take the long view, make up your minds to the end you wish, for we have only our own lives to live, and walk magnificently toward it." And then he could not help quoting what to me was the most beautiful thing that has ever been written: "We are such stuff as dreams are made on, and our little life is rounded with a sleep."

Everybody felt good and beautiful, including myself, and my stock in the school rose a hundred per cent.

I spent all the time with Mama that I could take from my lessons, even bringing my books up to her room and studying. She was failing, very sick indeed, and when I saw the look of pain and terror in her face and Sister Augusta sitting beside her, rubbing her forehead gently, her lips moving, but no sound coming, maybe in some Russian benediction, I put up my books and went over near Mama. I wanted every minute with her, every breath of her life that I could have. A nurse came to relieve Sister Augusta for part of the day.

Mama died in the night with Sister Augusta's hand in hers, and I was not there. I was asleep. Nothing told me that Mama was dying, and I could not understand God letting me sleep, with no sign, no warning, and I was angry.

We all wore mourning. Our old Mrs. Dunn came with her daughter to help, and they stayed up half the night to get the things finished. I was kept home from school, so I sewed with them. It was a strange time. I had thought that when Mama died my own life would end. I thought it would be impossible to exist. I had felt that the well-spring of our lives were one, that I was a piece of her, attached, and that when she died my own soul would bleed out and leave me drained.

It was October, warm and spicy, and Father Flannery took me up to stay in his house with Mrs. Dunn's daughter Marie to look after me. I wanted to go to the funeral, but Daddy said no, he would not have it; he could not bear even to see me in black; he thought it was barbarous. I did not mind the black; I liked it. It gave me a kind of comfort. They said a Mass for Mama in the church, and I went, and knelt down and felt holy in my mourning. My hands clasped before

me in black suède were far more effective than if I had
had on my everyday brown leather gloves, and I liked
people on the street to know by looking at me that I
mourned.

Father Flannery talked with me that night before
I went to bed. His voice was soft and kind and had a
persuasive quality to it that I had never heard before.
I told him how troubled I had been that the passing of
Mama's soul had not called me from my sleep.

"That is how it is," he said. "We must not question
God's ways. The soul flies up to Him, released from
its earthly circle. Your Mama was a celestial being as
she breathed her last. Greater heads than yours have
pondered, have tried to catch the evanescent spirit."

We were sitting in Father Flannery's study; his
green-shaded student lamp was the only light, and it
gave the room a lovely look that it did not have by day.
The housekeeper came in with cake and a decanter of
wine on a tray. It was solid yellow homemade cake
with raisins in it, and it gave me a good feeling. Here
were things I knew. I could see and touch and taste.
I took a bite of the cake and a mouthful of the wine.
The mingled flavours were delicious; so were the tex-
tures of the cake and raisins, and the wine softening
them in my mouth. Father Flannery was talking.

"There are things we know for certain, but we

183

know them in a way different from the way you are tasting Bridget's excellent cake." He was looking at me, much amused. He was a mighty smart man. "We know them through faith. I promised your Da that I would do nothing to try to bring you into the Church, not just now. I think I should not even try to comfort you, but let you grieve your grief out; it will be something to carry with you. You will enjoy your life, my lamb, that I can see. You'll always have your pack on your back. Some day, though," and he closed his eyes and folded his hands, and a wonderful look came over his face, a look that gave me more than all his words, "some day you will want more. You will know that the bread and the wine are only symbols. Some day the bread and the wine will lose their flavour for you, and you will long for Faith everlasting."

Father Chris brought me home the day after Mama's funeral. The house was strange. Her room had been cleared of all her things, and Sister Augusta was gone. She did not even leave good-bye for me, and I never saw her again. But her greatness stayed with me, like an indefinable star, something above and beyond my understanding.

Thirteen

De Forest tried his best to be nice to me after Mama's death. He asked me to go out for a drive with him in a victoria one afternoon. I liked the idea of going out for a drive through the park. I seldom went any more since Nana had no carriage, but when I thought of sitting with him all around the park, I must have shown my feeling in my face. He laughed and looked at Nana.

"No takee," he said, and although he smiled he was none too pleased, I could see. "I must be fallin' off when the young 'uns don't jump. I tell you, young lady, they wait in droves for me to throw the handkerchief."

"Now, Jack," said Nana, "she isn't entirely grown up yet, although her new dresses have long skirts."

"It isn't that, is it?" he asked me.

He knew I didn't like him, yet he wanted me to, not that he cared a bit that I should; it was his vanity, and I think he overestimated my influence with Nana. She asked me later if I would go out with him if he asked me again.

"As a favour to me, darling," she said, "things are none too easy nowadays, will you help me to make the best?"

I kissed her, and then held her very close. I was growing tall, almost as tall as she was, and I suddenly felt the older of the two of us. Father Flannery was right, there were things we knew through other channels than taste or sight or touch, and I knew her life then, as though I saw every action of it. She loved that man, in spite of herself, more than she had ever loved any other. It was a mystery, having known Tom Watson, but it was true.

I did go out with him one afternoon, only we had a brougham instead of a victoria. It was no pleasure for either of us. I knew there was something he wanted to tell me, but a stiffness grew up in me and we were almost home before he could talk. The shades of the carriage were not all the way up, and I pulled the little cord that released the spring on the window nearest me. The silk shade flew up as though it were alive, and it was such a sure wonderful action that I pulled it down and let it go up again. It relieved the tension.

"Delicious," he said, in a society voice, and I stopped immediately.

Then he told me that he was about to get a divorce, and if he could persuade Nana to marry him, he hoped that we were all going to be happy about it.

"No," I said, "I can never be happy about it, but so many things happen nowadays," and I began to cry.

"Now, come, try to think about your Nana instead of yourself. You're a very selfish little thing. You've been loved and petted and spoiled all your life, and it's about time somebody came along and put some sense into you."

I stopped crying and looked at him.

"It's Ray I love," he said. "I don't care a good God damn about you or any of you, but we might as well be comfortable about it."

"I hate the sight of you," I said, "and I only came out because she asked me to."

"Thank God you stopped crying. Jesus Christ, what would she think if I brought you home slobbering all over like that?"

He took out his linen handkerchief and tried to wipe my eyes and nose.

"Don't run away with the idea this is a treat for me. She wanted me to break the news, damn it."

He called out to the coachman to go slower.

"Now look here, we're almost home. Try to get your face in shape, and let's make up our minds to make the best of the bargain."

We had come out of the park entrance at Fifty-ninth Street and Fifth Avenue, and were going down Fifth and were about to turn west at Forty-fifth Street. I had two and a half long cross-town blocks to stop crying, and the horse was walking.

"All right," I said, although I wanted to indulge in a fine emotional outburst. I wanted to cry and carry on, and maybe slap his face or bite him. "I'll tell her we had a lovely time, and I'm glad you're going to be married. But—"

"No 'buts,' let's make a good go of it."

"But I'm not going to live with you. I'm—"

He threw his head back and laughed, and all the things I hated in him were laughing.

"That was never in the scheme. Ray and I are going away, clearing out. I—"

With that I let fly. I slapped his face and kicked his shins as hard as I could, and yelled in rage. The coachman stopped and came around to see what was the matter. Between them they got hold of my hands and feet and held me until I quieted down from the fit of rage.

He left me off at the house and did not come in.

Fortunately it was a matinee day and Daddy was playing. Nana was out, and there was nobody to see me except Amelia. She made me take a nice cup of hot tea, and she told me that you never could tell but what it was all for the best.

"Yo aunty she's plum crazy about him, an' what mo' can a woman want than to be livin' with a man she's plum crazy for, even if it las's only a while? Cain't ask no mo' of life than that!"

I hadn't thought about Nana's happiness. I had only thought of myself, and I was ashamed.

Fortunately I had a lot of work to do. Examinations were coming in June, and I was way behind in a lot of subjects. I saw more of Daddy. He was free of the girl called Aggie, or whoever she was. She might have had a successor. On Saturdays I went down to the theatre where he was playing, watched some of the show, and we walked home together for dinner. I always loved the back of the theatre. I liked to sit in the wings on a rickety chair and look at the performers; looking at them from that point of view was entirely different from seeing them from the front, as though they had a different dimension. All the exaggeration of their acting showed up, yet it had an extraordinary quality of artistry, the essence of life. You could see so clearly what they meant—love and hate were love and hate threefold. Nobody knows the greatest beauty of acting until he sees it from the wings. In a way, I learned how to look at objects, too, though I looked at them from there, framed off from the ordinary, placed somewhere in my own dream of them.

Daddy was taking off his make-up, and I was sitting beside his dressing-table. I asked him if he thought Mama would like it or not if I was an actress. He was taking great gobs of petroleum jelly from a square tin, rubbing it on his face, and wiping off the grease paint with a piece of an old towel that was the colour of brick dust. His face looked fresh and young as a baby's after the Vaseline cleansing, but his hair was grey and the crow's-feet around his eyes had grown deep. He had been laughing at something when I asked him, but he stopped and looked at me seriously. His red and gold costume was hanging on the wall behind him, his shoes, with their gay diamond buckles and red heels, were just in front of me on the floor, and his fantastic, curled grey wig was on a wig-stand. He had on a grey silk Japanese kimono, and the walls and mirror were all pinned and stuck with photographs and telegrams since his opening. He was playing the Duke of Plaza Toro, and he was the handsomest thing you ever saw when he came out in his beautiful costume.

He looked quietly at me, then leaned over with his arms on the dressing-table and looked at his face in the mirror.

"It's a dreadful life," he said. "Too hard for a girl like you. Your dear Mama never said anything to me about it, but I know what I think, darling," and he began to pat witch hazel over his face and dusted it with powder. "I would hate to see you do it. I wish I could be a stern parent and say I forbid it. That's how strongly I feel. You know, if you are an actress there are certain kinds of life that will be closed to you, certain sections of society, and you are so—"

"Oh, Daddy," I said, "I'll never be anything but an actor's daughter. That is what I was born to, and I don't want anything else. All I want is the chance to be able to—oh, how can I say what I want? I want to be able to tell people how I feel about things, in a different way from real life."

"There are more ways than acting to do that," he said.

But at the same time he could not help himself. He acted in the mirror; he made masks of his face as he had done for me when I was little; he made a comic face and a grotesque face, sentimental and tragic faces.

"And this face," he said, "is the face of a swell society chap who has taken a dose of salts and somebody else is occupying the water-closet." And he made a face that was so strained the blood coloured it and a sickly smile forced up the corners of his mouth.

"That's a funny way to keep me from wanting to act," I said, "but it's a wonderful way to make me love you a lot."

"We'll go see Tom Watson one of these days and see what he has to say about it."

We went one afternoon. It was getting on toward the end of June. It was one of those wonderful days when the whole city was sparkling. Daddy had on his black and white pin check suit, with a pearl-grey bow tie, and he wore his straw sailor for the first time that season. He looked gay, and as we walked down Broadway together I felt so good, so happy, and so strong that I did not care whether they decided I should be an actress or not. Anything seemed good so long as I could walk down Broadway with Daddy, listen to him talk and see him smile, and say hello to all the actors who were standing around. I was out of mourning. Mrs. Dunn had made me a fawn-coloured dress, ankle-length; the belt and collar were made of Dresden ribbon, and I had a big bow at the back of my neck like those the ladies were wearing that year.

Coming into Tom Watson's place was like a different world. It was dark, and the handsome bronze cases were ranged along the walls, holding their pieces of timeless beauty. Miss Cullen, his secretary, showed us into the inner office; her manner was perfect, but I am sure it was quite different from the manner she used with the buying clients when she ushered them in.

The two men talked awhile about the shows that were closing, what kind of season it had been, and what was in the offing.

"Uncertain life, isn't it, Joe?" said Tom Watson, "but not much more uncertain than the Chinese porcelain business. You put a pile of money into a jar, thinking some of these men will fall over one another bidding for it. There it is for eighteen months now, eating its head off in a glass case." He pointed to a cabinet holding a single vase, a huge graceful jar painted blue on white with the story of the life of a princess, a life of palaces, pavilions, waiting women, lovers on horses, and twining flowers, in an endless pattern.

"That's what I am telling this child of mine," said Daddy. "She wants to go on the stage. She wants to tell people something. Well, darling, you'd better tell him yourself what you want to do."

I told him that I did not want to go to school any more; that I could never be a teacher, which was what most of my classmates were aiming to be; in fact, it was the only job that was possible for a girl. Daddy told him that we came to talk things over with him.

"You know, Tom, what an actress's life is like. I guess she thinks she knows about it too," and Daddy put out his hand and took mine, and kissed my fingers, "but there's an awful lot you have never dreamed of, honey. Still, she has to be ready to look after herself some day. What do you think, Tom?"

The sapphire-blue eyes were looking about the room, resting on some of the beautiful porcelains, maybe looking for an answer in them. I followed his eyes, and some of the answer began to dawn on me. Some unknown creator, centuries back, was telling us, sitting there in that cool room, how he felt about things, about hawthorn branches against the sky, the full-throated song of birds, princesses having tea in fairy palaces, and the ecstasy of flowers. Our eyes met, and I nodded.

He took a pair of spectacles out of his pocket and put them on; I had never seen the spectacles before. He was heavier, and his face was white, and he had not once tried to rise from his chair while we were there. Still, he was more like himself than ever, and held more of what I wanted in life than anybody I had ever known. His hand with the emerald signet turned the letters over on his desk.

"It seems to me I remember some drawings a long time ago. I liked them at the time. Here, this is what I am looking for." He took a large square envelope from the pile. "I've been elected president of something, a school of design, a very good one, and along with the honour I am asked to give a scholarship. Now, this is an idea, why not try a term in October? There will be plenty of time to change if it is not a good idea. We can find paints and brushes and papers; maybe it will be a channel for some of this fine feeling."

My hands were in my lap, relaxed and quiet. As he spoke, I could feel a tingling life. My fingers felt as I think the twigs of trees must feel when the first green feathery leaves break through; all of my life came to my hands and my fingers.

"I'll do what I can with them," I said, holding up my hands toward him.

"That's it," he said, and he took my right hand and shook it. "Shall we say yes?"

He wanted to send over to the Union League Club for tea, but Daddy had an engagement. I think it must have been an engagement at the Barrett House bar for something else than tea. When five o'clock came and Daddy was not in that bar, it meant either he was rehearsing, or the end of the world had come. We got up to go, and Miss Cullen came in to see us out. Daddy went into the front show-room with her. Tom Watson sat still in his chair.

I knew he had something more to say; so I went over and stood beside him. He took both my hands this time and looked up at me with that strangely humorous expression of his that I have never seen since in a human face.

"I don't like playing providence, but your father asked it of me. If you are a Bernhardt, it will out; no art school will thwart you. I am not one to tell you which is the better life, let me only ask you to try. You won't be married to this drawing business. Possibly before the final choice comes you will be married to a husband; that would make us all happy. Will you tell your dear aunty what I have said? Is she well, is she happy?"

I did not know what to say, I did not know if he knew or not that she intended marrying De Forest.

"She's pretty well, you know Nana, and I think she's happy, sort of. She's looking very lovely," I could not help saying; maybe it was the wrong thing, for he let go of my hands and started to get up.

"Give her this message for me," he said; "tell her that I wish her well, never anything but that no matter what she may think, and tell her that I appoint myself your unofficial guardian. That may give her some comfort when she needs it most."

I could not bear to leave him, to go from the quiet of his office, from the quality of his presence, to the troubles of home. I realized that he had let Nana go, and that in letting her go she had clutched at what was near, and what was near had drawn her in and down, until she was absorbed.

Walking up home I went over in my mind again and again how I was going to tell her where we had been and what he had said. I left Daddy at the Barrett House, at the swinging doors of the barroom, and I wished I was a man. A pungent odour came out, fresh wet sawdust and rye whisky, bitters and lemon peel, and the bitter smell of beer. Somebody was playing an accordion, and they had all shifted their burdens onto nothingness.

As I walked up the stoop I noticed that the front door was partly opened. I hurried in, with a sudden feeling that something was happening; burglars were my first guess. A lot of hats were in the hall, and it seemed like a lot of people in the parlour. Nana was standing near the door, looking white and shaky, Mrs. Elsom was next to her, crying and making a lot of noise, and the rest of them were strange men. The two men that I used to see at Mrs. Elsom's place were there, and several others, all talking to her.

"Now about that sapphire and diamond ring, Mrs. Greenfield," one of them was asking; "all I want is facts. When did you buy it, and how much did you pay for it?"

I felt a sick feeling at the pit of my stomach, the same as I felt when the one called Jeff almost touched me. I was afraid of what she was going to say, she had worn the ring for almost a year and it was gone now, I knew it, for I had missed it among her things.

"It was given to me for a present, how can I tell how much was paid for it?"

"Will you let me see it?" said a youngish-looking man; he was thin and tall, with a sandy moustache and clear green eyes; his voice was rather kind, and I wished with all my heart that she would tell him the truth, for he was going to get it out of her anyway.

She looked at him, and I could see that she was going to make the best try she knew how. She relaxed, she took off the tension like taking off the tissue-paper wrappings from a parcel. Her hands went through her hair, she took a step forward, and the slanting smile lit her face like an incandescent light.

"Somebody who cared for me a great deal felt that he could make me happy with that ring," she said; "it did give me a lot of pleasure for a while, I liked to see it on my finger," and she put her hand on the back of the same chair that his hand was holding. Everybody in the room looked at her, as though the ring would appear from the air on her finger.

"But I—but things were different, but I—"

The young man with the green eyes put his hand in his pocket and held up the ring for all of us to see. "Is this it?"

No doubt he had seen me come in, but he had only noticed me when the question of the ring came up and he seemed to be asking me the question direct.

"Never seen it, so 'elp me," shouted Mrs. Elsom, and Jeff gave her a poke and she was quiet.

"Yes," said Nana, "it looks like my ring. Where did you get it?"

"It was pawned by a Mr. John Smith, about a week ago, at Macneely's shop on Sixth Avenue, and corresponds to the description of a ring missing from Tiffany's since June 26th of last year. The broker describes this Smith as a handsome man, very well dressed in black coat and striped trousers, signet ring on right little finger."

"That's our ring," said an oldish man, looking as frightened as I felt.

My heart was in my throat, for I recognized the description of Smith. Mrs. Elsom shrieked and made a dash for the door. Green eyes had Jeff cornered, and another young man grabbed Mrs. Elsom.

Jeff sidled over to Nana. "You must know a tidy lot of gentlemen, you'd never let a friend like me get into trouble," he said; "it might be trouble all around."

"Come now," said the man with the green eyes, his name was Osborne I found out later, "we'll try to straighten this out ourselves, no interference."

Then he went on to tell her that they knew all about the ring and who was responsible for the disposal of it, if not the theft, although he was pretty certain. "But what I would like to clear up is this," he said, and he looked concerned, as though he did not like what he was doing; "I would like to know how your friend, who made you the gift, came by this ring, for I presume you must know something about it."

"It is not my habit," she said in a voice much too sure, "to ask where my presents are bought. I either accept them or not, as I choose." But the lace on the front of her dress trembled as though the room was swept with breezes, and the knuckles on the hand holding the chair were white.

Osborne told the man who had hold of Jeff to take him and Mrs. Elsom and the other chap around to Mrs. Elsom's shop. "Might as well go quietly," he said to her, lighting up a cigarette, "it will go harder with you if you try to run out. I'll follow."

Osborne gathered up his papers and went out into the hall to get his hat. Nana was weak from the tension; she still had hold of the chair back, and her eyes were shut; it looked as though she was going to faint. She might have, only Osborne came back into the room and she straightened up again.

"Now that they are gone, Mrs. Greenfield, suppose we have a little talk. I am sure that if you will be frank with me we can save time, and future trouble. We know that Mrs. Elsom's shop is a fence, and that the two men here keep her supplied. But so far we do not know who does the thieving. I did not like to ask you this before the rest of them, but how did you come to lose your ring, when did you miss it, why did you not inform the police, and have you any idea who is this man Smith who pawned it?"

He sat down on a chair, quite pleasantly, and I must say he was an engaging person. He turned in my direction.

"It may be simpler if the young lady—" and he looked then at Nana.

"I hope Mrs. Elsom isn't going to have a terrible time," I said "she's so nice, and so jolly sometimes; it's those two men. I'm sure she's frightened of them."

"Better go upstairs, pet. Where's your Daddy?"

I left them. Not that I really wanted to, but I was

afraid of Osborne, afraid that I would tell him everything I knew about Mrs. Elsom. That man could have
got the truth out of me in no time. He did, finally,
from Nana, and it took him only about half an hour.
She was afraid that De Forest would get into trouble,
for she had sent him to pawn the ring herself. He was
not to blame, and if he had known where the ring
came from he would have had more sense than to have
gone to a pawnshop with it. The affair was a shock to
her. She had lived her life in the belief that everything
would always turn out right for her. They let Mrs.
Elsom off; but Jeff and the other man got two years at
Sing Sing; much as I hated them, I felt badly to think
that anybody I had known and actually spoken to
should lose his liberty.

The neighbourhood got wind of the trouble, and
soon all the tradesmen were around like birds of prey
after their bills. Jake the fishman did what he could,
short of paying the bills himself, and that would have
been too much for a man far richer than he was. Nana
had not paid her tailor or her dressmaker or her de-
partment-store bills for ages. It seemed incredible that
people could be so trusting. Small fractions of bills
had been paid once in a while, but at longer and longer
intervals. Jake was a brick, and it was he who called

the creditors together in our dining-room one evening and arranged a settlement.

"You can't get money from where no money is," he said; "you should all have enough experience to know that. I've tried it myself and it don't work. Now, our friend Mrs. Greenfield here, she owns this elegant furniture, the rugs and the carpets and all these grand ornaments, and she's willing to sell them, every stick and shred, for the benefit of her creditors. Now, is that a fine woman or is it?"

They almost cheered but not quite. It had a fine sound, but no doubt some of them knew how little there would be from the sale of second-hand furniture, and that little divided among so many. Amelia came in with a big glass pitcher of beer; she must have bought it with her own money. "Cain't bear it," said Amelia when Nana asked her about the beer; "so many gents talkin' their heads off for so long, without no refreshment."

We never saw the auction in the house, as it was planned. Somebody told Louis Greenfield about it. I would not be surprised if it was Jake; for all his kindness, Jake would not have been averse to having his bill settled in full.

Louis paid up everybody, and offered Daddy to look

after me if he would send me to boarding-school. But Daddy and I could manage; besides I was going to art school in October. Some of our relations wanted to take my little sister, but we had already arranged with Father Flannery to send her to the nuns' school, in a lovely old convent in Bronx Park.

Fourteen

I went away to the country for the breaking up of
the household. I stayed with some actor friends of
Daddy's who had a place on the Jersey coast, in Long
Branch; it was run as a sort of roadhouse and restaurant. It was a rainy week, and I was blue and sad, and
frightfully homesick; sick for a home that would never
be again. They were as nice to me as they could be,
and under other circumstances I should have had a
splendid time. Kitty and Jerry Jackson both sang,
they had been a good team, and we all three sang together in the evenings.

"Very sweet voice," said Kitty.

"Very small voice," said Jerry.

"It can be built up," said Kitty.

"Maybe," said Jerry.

"Nothing carries a voice over better than a pair of
pretty eyes," said Kitty.

"Nothing carries a voice over better than a pair of
pretty legs," said Jerry.

"Or a small red mouth," said Kitty.

"Or a small round waist," said Jerry.

"Or a fine head of curly hair," said Kitty.

"Or the way she could walk across the stage and give them the look at the exit."

That was how they were being as nice to me as they could. We always went to bed laughing, no matter how down I had been feeling in the daytime. Fortunately there was a lot to do; they were getting the place ready for the summer, and I was glad to help with painting the outdoor furniture and the porch. They taught me how to make their specialty, a clam chowder made of soft long-necked clams, with sage and whole black peppercorns cooked in it. Also a delicious biscuit with bacon crumbled up in it. They were doing well in a modest way, and hoped to branch out in another year. They had put all their savings into the place, owned it free and clear, so they would have a home. "Look at me now," said Kitty; "how would I look as Cupid? I'm getting beyond burlesque size."

Kitty was fat, her face was the colour of a peony, and her hair was the colour of the big French horn in the Long Branch Band. "Time enough to let it go grey after we have the first hundred thousand in the bank."

I had her picture in my collection. She was a lovely

little thing, all tender curves, dressed in pink fleshings that came up to her neck, down to her wrists and ankles, and she wore pink satin trunks and a rakish little cap. A pair of spangled wings were on her shoulders, she carried a tinsel bow and arrow, and her eyes were bound with a wisp of gauze. You'd never have known her for the same.

They wanted me to stay with them for the summer, and it was tempting; for I knew I could have done enough for them to earn my board. When Daddy came down to fetch me home, he told me he had arranged for us to live for a while with one of his sisters who had a big house uptown, with a whole floor we could have for ourselves. He was not looking awfully well; some of the brilliance had gone from his face, and his eyes were puffy. I thought I had better go with him.

"Only until my ship comes in," he said, for he saw that the idea of living with my aunt was not very welcome to me. "Then we'll have a flat down near Madison Square. I have it picked out already, and—"

"With Amelia in it?" I asked.

"Yes, Amelia in it, and a studio with a big window, and when they send for you to come down to the White House to paint Grover Cleveland's portrait, your old Daddy will put on his galoshes and ear muffs, grasp his crutches, and come along."

"Sounds like a long way off."

"There's a lot to do between," he said. "Now, pet, how do you feel, do you feel strong?"

"You know I'm as strong as a horse."

"Well, you need to be. I have some news for you, and please don't topple over. I've got a letter too," and he took it out of his pocket.

A million things flashed through my head, and the right thing came uppermost, and stuck.

"They've married!" I said.

"By the Mayor, in City Hall, and your Daddy was best man. Nana wanted you there; he didn't want anybody, but she insisted on having me. Now, now, pet," for I couldn't help feeling a little badly.

"Oh," I wailed, "not to be there when she was married, even to that son of a bitch."

He laughed loud, and soon we were both laughing.

"She isn't dead, you know," he said, "read your letter."

It was a moving letter, though she was no writer, and it had lots of mistakes, mostly grammatical; but it was full of the feeling that was Nana.

. . . and after we come back from a trip to Virginia we will have a house down somewhere in New Jersey

and you must come every week, I want to watch you grow. Joe tells me you are going to get a flat as soon as he can afford it, and then if you want me, I will come to New York once in a while and see that your ears are kept clean, and maybe go to Delmonico's for a swell dinner. From all accounts I hear the dinners are pretty fair in Jersey too. Now be a good girl and try to be happy, but I know you will be, you can't help it. I hope, I know, that you will want me to be happy too, and I am now, only I wish I had you two dear children nearer.

Your loving Nana

And it was incredible how soon I was happy again. We had a splendid floor in my other aunty's house. There wasn't much fun in that house, but I was absorbed in my work at art school, and Daddy took me out with him a great deal at night. We went to theatres and to the opera whenever he could get tickets, even to prize fights. Only the toughest females went to fights, and they needed to be; after two I begged off, although there were certain things that were interesting to me. I was studying anatomy. The men's bodies were beautiful, and it was fascinating to watch the play of muscles under their sweaty skins, muscles that had been cold difficult names for me until I saw them moving in the fight. But the sound of the impact of fist against flesh was sickening. It thudded into the pit of my stomach and made me feel faint; maybe it was the atmosphere too, thick with smoke and human smells; maybe it was the expression on the faces of the crowd. I was afraid at how much they enjoyed it, and I didn't want to get to enjoy it myself.

We went to see our star, who was giving a repertory season of his old successes. I wanted to see his Richard, to recapture its strange dread. Daddy got seats in the front row because he had invited aunty to go with us and she was quite deaf. It could not have been so many years since we had been in London with him, but it was a lifetime for me, I had grown from childhood into something else. He wanted to see us, and he asked Daddy to bring me backstage before the performance as he had to go out to a party afterwards. I had grown tall enough to be almost a woman's level to his man's height. I wore skirts to my ankles, my hair was in a knot at my neck, and he barely knew me.

"My little prince is gone," he said, looking closely at my face, while he held his cosmetic tin over the candle, "but, Joe, can it be that I will find the leading lady I've been searching for all these years?"

"No," said Daddy, "we talked it over, and she's going to art school; we'll see how it works out."

"When I'm awfully good, I'll paint your Richard, but how can it possibly be as good as you?"

His dresser had put a chair for me beside the dressing-table; it was as wonderful as ever to watch him again, putting on the sickly clammy hue of distaste, the lines of cruelty in the face, and the horrid mauve lips. But we had to leave before I saw him do the hunchback walk from his dressing-room to the wings, that most perfect touch of his characterization.

I had been looking forward all day to the small time before the rise of the curtain, when the house was dark and the footlights spilled up on the plush, and you could hear the click of the ropes just as the curtain rose.

He was standing crooked, in a crooked London street, one shoulder up, matching the aged crookedness of the half-timber slanting house. Enter Richard, Duke of Gloucester, solus. He was turned semi-profile, until the applause rippled over him, then he walked downstage, the slow loping fearful walk. He paused, and turned in thought. "Now is the winter of our discontent—"

"Made bright," whispered Daddy.

"Shh," I whispered back.

The play proceeded. It went on and on to deeds of horror; betrayals, slanders, murders, executions, until I felt I could bear no more. Another murder, another

bloody sword, and I would have to leave. As he spoke
the nightmare scene in his tent, the scene changed before my eyes. I was standing on a beach, facing a blue
and shining sea. The sun beat back from the sand into
my eyes, and the atmosphere moved in waves of heat. I
heard the sound of hoofs, distant poundings that might
have been the echoes of my own heart-beats. I looked
to my right, and in the distance a chariot was coming
toward me, first a tiny speck in a golden cloud of sand,
growing larger as it came swiftly near me. The car of
the chariot was wood, silver grey from the salt sea air,
the colour of driftwood, and bound with metal. Three
grey horses thundered on the wet sand, driven by a
woman. Her right hand held the white reins; her left
hand rested on the shoulder of a young girl, and a little
boy stood at her other side, just tall enough to look over
the rim of the car. They were all in a diaphanous cream
colour, the children had gold fillets on their heads, but
the woman's hair was bound round and round with a
magenta ribbon. A cape of the same delicate material
as her dress floated out in the air behind her; she was
straight and strong, the loveliest thing I ever saw, the
womanliest woman. In a flash she was past and the
vision was ended, save that the hoof-beats sounded in
my heart until they had gone, too. I must have half
risen in my seat, for Daddy was pulling at my hand.

It could have lasted only a few seconds, for with the last of the sound, Richard was finishing a sentence he had begun. I could still smell the salt air and feel the sunny wind from the chariot as it passed me. It was perfection.

Richard ended the tragedy of his wretched life. He was better than ever, and walking up the aisle I felt sorry that I was not going to be part of the noble profession, and I wished that they had let me decide for myself what I wanted to do.

Aunty was looking glum. "Well," she said, "they're all dead but the orchestra. I wish they'd play something else but *Hail, Columbia* when you walk out of the theatre. Now I hope you didn't pay for the tickets, did you, Joe?" But she couldn't spoil it for me, nobody could.

The St. Nicholas Skating Rink was turned into a concert hall in the summer-time. A man named Kaltenborn was the director of the orchestra; he was a good violinist and had fine musical taste. Daddy and I went about three times a week, and usually Father Flannery and Father Chris came along. It was a real musical education, and those evenings were almost the most pleasant I ever knew in my life. When the music was over, we went round the corner to Healy's for a drink and talk. They had beer, and I had Rhine wine and seltzer, unless Father Flannery felt good and ordered champagne all around. He loved it; so did I. There were certain pieces of music that called for it, he said.

"You can't wash down the 'Romeo and Juliet' with anything but champagne, not unless you're a callous soul. Now I can take six seidels of dark beer after the Rhine music," and he took out his watch and put it on the table. It was quarter past eleven, and they had three quarters of an hour to drink. At twelve to the dot they stopped, for Mass had to be said on an empty stomach. We had just been listening to the Tchaikovsky music. That music was myself, it was all the young, tender, yet fierce passion I had never known; it played on the bud of my life like the strong summer sun, and I could feel my life expanding in circles of bliss. My mind, body, and senses were a resolved chord, and out of the chord I broke into other harmonies, and I had a vision of endless combinations, broken and livened by the pop of the champagne cork. Father Flannery had wonderful ideas. It was his marvellous sense of life that made him the great priest he was.

We were sitting at a large round table in a corner of the restaurant, almost surrounded by wine-coolers. They wanted plenty on hand, against the twelve o'clock signal. Mr. Healy himself came up and had a glass with us, and a friend of Daddy's came in, they had some sort of date together for the end of the evening. I had had two or three glasses of champagne by that time, the lights were twinkling in the globes and on the varnished panelling, and the violin solo a man was playing in the grill room had a singularly piercing quality. However, nothing was so singular as the way this friend of Daddy's was dressed. I thought maybe it was the wine that made me think it strange, along with the emotions induced by "Romeo and Juliet."

This man, John Feemster, was an Irishman, a big ruddy raw-boned man, with sandy hair and beard. He was a champion whisky-drinker, and the whisky did not make him bloated and fat; it gave him the look of a country squire who spends his life in the open, on horses, mahogany-coloured from the elements. He didn't go on sprees; he nibbled on a whisky bottle all day long and all night, like an infant with a rubber pacifier. He had bottles of whisky all over his studio, and in his bedroom, and always in his pocket when he went out. He had run away from home in Belfast, where his father had a textile business. He didn't want to live his life turning out tablecloths and napkins and counting up the profits, he wanted to be a painter. Now he was counting up his profits in New York, for he was designing and manufacturing a handsome tooled leather for walls, the same as Tom Watson had in his back office, and there wasn't a house on Fifth Avenue that did not have at least two of his rooms and a few of his screens.

He had on a garment of grey linen, cut like a butcher's coat, or one of the coats a fur merchant wears at work, very long and wide; gauntlet gloves with black leather cuffs, and a cap of the same grey linen. Against his forehead was what looked like two great white-rimmed eyes, which proved to be a monstrous pair of spectacles that he had pushed up. What's more, there was another one, came in right after him, smaller, but dressed exactly the same; and with a very dirty face.

"Sorry to be late, Joe. I've had the time of my life. I've bought one of those contraptions, and you've all got to come out with me."

He looked around over his shoulder. "Here's young Wilbur, he sort of came with the machine, he's its nurse, can't walk without him. What are you, Wilbur, are you my hired man or my secretary, or my companion or what? He's been my best friend for the last five hours, haven't you, m'lad?"

Wilbur took off his cap and from the sweat band up he was a blondish chap. Grease and dirt had settled into every pore of his face and hands.

"Don't tell me you've put good Irish-American

money into a horseless carriage," said Father Flannery, "with the stable full of grand horseflesh you have."

"Stableful eating their heads off; while all young Wilbur here has to do is open a cock and give the damn thing a drink of oil."

"And chug-chug, off we go," I said, feeling high.

"Sometimes," said young Wilbur, "but the little place I got here," and he opened his mouth and put his forefinger in it, "needs steak."

It was half past eleven; while Feemster and Wilbur went to the wash-room, we ordered them a steak cooked rare. "Brown on the outside and just heated through," said Father Flannery to the waiter; "he likes it bloody."

Wilbur was a nice-looking boy when he was clean, and could put away an enormous amount of steak. We all watched the clock for our last glass of champagne, and at midnight to the dot, Daddy banged his fist on the table and said: "Done!" Wilbur put the piece of steak that was left between two slices of bread; Feemster took two bottles of whisky, and we went out to Columbus Avenue.

The automobile was standing at the curb; it was a handsome machine, painted grey, with red leather upholstery, and lots of shiny brass. It was like a miniature Fifth Avenue bus without the top. Three brass-bound steps went up to the little door at the back, and seats faced each other the length of the car. Wilbur took the wheel, and Feemster got in beside him in the front seat. The rest of us got in the back, and sat while Wilbur turned things on and off, got in and out several times, grunted and swore, then got the thing started and the vibration made my teeth chatter. We were off, in a deafening sound.

East on Sixty-sixth Street, in the park and around. Up beyond Seventy-second Street the machinery stopped and we waited. Wilbur got underneath, came out again and said he didn't know, the thing had been going all day long, and here we were.

"Maybe she's thirsty," said Feemster.

"Or hungry," said Father Flannery; "where's that steak sandwich you took along, lad, any of ye got some oats and a bale of hay?"

"Ye-haw, ye-haw," said Daddy, "neigh-h-h-h."

We had all got out. It was cool and moist and beautiful, and the darkness of the night was like a dream.

A policeman came up to see if we were in trouble. He started to shout at us: "Ye'll be wakin' up the worrums, that thing snortin' and kickin', who are ye to be—" Then he saw the clerical collars and almost fainted. "Holy father, ridin' around against providence!"

"Have a drop," said Feemster, holding out his bottle. The officer had a drop.

"Everything has a beginning, oncet," said the officer.

"Meaning you never had a drop before?" said Feemster.

"Meaning somebody must oncet have taken the first roid in a steam cyar and a steam boat, and a—and a—"

"That's it," I said, "we're making history."

The thing gave a snort and a bang and started vibrating. We all got in again and Wilbur started her going fast, so fast that my hat blew off; I didn't care, I said we would look for it on the way back, I had the makings of another hat at home, a natural straw, I screamed, only nobody heard me, for the wind, and I screamed I was going to trim it with a red geranium. The wind blew into my mouth and nostrils and nearly choked me, and my hair whipped around my face and into my eyes. The engine was running perfectly, and we rolled around the park, in the black beautiful night. Even if he had heard me, Wilbur wouldn't have stopped to look for my hat. We had been all around the park for we passed the policeman, and he waved to us, maybe to stop, maybe only in greeting. We went on and on, round and round the park, for we passed him again and again. We dashed out to Amsterdam Avenue to get some petrol to put in the engine, and Daddy and Feemster finished Feemster's bottle while Wilbur was waking up his friend in the hardware store. I was getting cold, so they gave me a nip, and it made me dozy, for I barely remember going on again, then my eyes opened to the velvet blackness, it was a blackness that was not only deep but round, not only a blackness to see but to feel. I put out my white handkerchief to see how white it would look in the black light, and let the wind whip it along, and it made the blackness even blacker. Then the wind took my handkerchief and blew it over the bushes and into a tree and then it was gone.

The two priests and Daddy and Wilbur were only shapes, yet I could distinguish them; they had stopped their singing and talking and were drunk as I was with the speed and the wind and the blackness. I raised my hands and the wind went through them as though I was dragging them from a boat, in water, then I fantasied that maybe I was drowning, my sins and my goodness all jumbled together, for I did not know which was which; then they came clear, all centred in my love for Nana. I had not gone to see Nana, I had not gone for my sins in hating her husband. Tomorrow, I told myself. Now, I told myself, and I shrieked to Wilbur to take me to Nana, now, but how could he hear? My voice was carried back; maybe the sound never got beyond my throat. I closed my eyes and gave myself to the flow of air and space and time, and with a great wrench my mind was separated from the thousand smallnesses that held it down, my new straw hat and the food and the drink, my dresses and the way I thought I should look, the way I thought people thought about me, the way those thoughts darted in and out of my larger concerns and kept me from the fullness of my power, the way when I was drawing a long steady line, beautiful as I could make it, from the top of the model's head down her shoulder and thigh and foot, my evil mind darted off to the codfish cakes my aunty had for breakfast, with a fried egg on top and the soft yolk mingling in delicious flavours with the fish; and my hand trembled and the cleanliness had gone from my line. Never any more, no, no more of those little things, I always have this night, this black perfection, flying through the park, cleansed of petty sin by the wind. I had Daddy with me, and the priests, whom I loved, and I had Nana with me already, tomorrow.

The speed was slowing and we stopped. Now there were two policemen, and the one we knew was waving a lantern. The big blackness had gone from the night, and a sense of light, no more, had crept over what objects I could see. The clouds shifted and broke, and ages away, in the space beyond the clouds, glittered a star, and the tip edge of the crescent of a moon, against the supreme colour of dawn. Sounds woke up in the trees, chirps and mutterings, and the airy sounds of wings, early morning sounds; nothing is so early as the sound of birds, they made a crown of sound around my head. Colour crept into things, slowly the trees came green and the policemen's coats came blue, and the honey-sweet breath of the leaves at dawn crept around us. We couldn't speak, any of us.

But the policemen could, both at once, and we made out that we were disturbing the peace and must come to the station house.

"What," said Wilbur, "on foot?"

"No," said the new policeman, "you come along in that noisy hell's wagon. We told the sergeant about it and he said we were liars."

"No disrespect," said our policeman, "but maybe first we can find a conveyance to take the reverend fathers home and maybe the young miss. Then we'll see about you chaps."

"Wait a little," said Father Flannery, "let us take a few quiet breaths and enjoy the beginning of a green new day. There are duties to be done, I have my own, and you have yours, and not too much time to spare.

First let us all join in our great duty, our thankfulness to God for His goodness in letting us see a new day, with love in our hearts."

We got out of the back of the car, and all of us stood there in the road, stretching beyond us on either side, very white in the light, and Father Flannery said a prayer in Latin, Father Chris saying it with him, then Feemster and the two policemen crossed themselves, and I did too. I thought it necessary and fitting.

There was no more talk of the station house, and there was no more go in the carriage; it was bone dry. We were near the West Side entrance where we had come in, not far from our house. We said good-bye to Feemster and Wilbur and left them arguing, and we walked to Columbus Avenue and found a hack for the two priests.

"Good night, Father Flannery," I said.

"Good night, child, ye crossed yourself, I noticed."

"Yes, I felt good, it was the birds and the trees, mostly the dawn."

"Ye're learning," he said; "it's in everything, it's life itself."

They left us, and we walked home. Daddy was not steady on his feet, he was still a little drunk. We stood on our stoop. He fumbled in his pocket for his keys, and I had to help him. It was a long journey up the stairs to our third floor, and when he came to his room he was very ill. I got him undressed and on his bed, and he was ill again; he was gasping and I was frightened. "Doctor," he breathed. I raced down to call aunty, and met the housemaid on the stairs. I told her to go down the block quick for the doctor, and I came back to Daddy, kneeling down beside his bed, and held him close.

I held his hand, and held his wonderful head against my shoulder, for a long, long time, but I could not hold life from leaving. People were in the room, and the doctor was talking to me and I realized he was telling me that Daddy had died, but I could not move my arms away.

They raised me up from the floor, and the doctor helped me into my room. Could this be, could the world end for me, and me so young? I felt as though I had swallowed misery, and it was a cold bitter rod in my middle. The doctor tried to get me to my bed, but I stood in the room and looked at everything around me. The new straw hat and the geranium were on the table, and my thimble and sewing things were catching the morning sun. I had a strong desire to stamp on the hat and the bright red flower, and I moved quickly to the table and took them in my hands. The petals of the flower were velvet; it was rich and beautiful, with its two round green leaves, and my hand put it where I would have sewed it, and it was lovely.

"He'll never see it," I sobbed to the doctor, "never, never. Oh, what am I going to do?"

"You're going to take this nice sugar pill I have for you and go to bed and get some sleep," he said. He had been only a sign to me till now, on a window in a brownstone house down near Central Park West, Brooks Fellowes, M.D. He was a man about forty, slightly grey at the temples, with a wonderful soothing quality. He got a glass of water and gave me the pill, and when I had taken off my dress and put on my wrapper he came into the room again and put a quilt over me.

He talked to me in a singsong quiet voice. I could not distinguish what he said; I was worn out, but the feeling and the effect were wonderful, for I soon fell asleep.

Nana was with me. Was it today, was it tomorrow, when I had said I would go to her? It was now, I had jumped out of sleep calling Nana, and she was standing beside the bed looking down at me. My strong quick body like a metal spring was on its feet, and then I went all soft and clung to her.

"Your Nana's here, pet; no one else can love you as much now." She petted my head and I buried my face in her shoulder; but it did not smell so sweet as it used to, and the hand on my cheek was not so soft, and it had a kitchen smell.

"You're going to come and live with your Nana now, will you?" she asked. "You can be a great help to me; we need each other."

Then I told her about the ride in the park, and how at the end I wanted her and called her name into the beautiful darkness.

"Something in you must have known," she said; "it happens that way."

She helped me dress, and I showed her the hat I was going to trim to wear to Daddy's birthday party next week; now there would be no party, and my heart came up and choked my throat and we both had a long cleansing cry. She told me about her house, a nice new small house with a garden. Amelia had helped her move down and settle in, but Amelia couldn't stand the country. She said it gave her the jitters, so "She sent her niece down to do the housework, but she can't cook, so I do now," and Nana held her hands out for me to see their roughness. They were not manicured, and they trembled as she tried to hold them out straight. I knew what that meant, and I said: "Nana!"

"I'm doing my best, pet. You don't know how good

he is to me, and how hard I try. Are you going to be an angel and come and help me too? I've missed you so. You can come in to art school every day on the train, and I'm sure there are nice young people living in the neighbourhood."

I was standing at the bureau brushing my hair, and she took the brush out of my hand and started to brush my hair herself.

"Maybe your friend Mr. Feemster will ride out to see you. I'd like to meet him," and she stopped brushing my hair and smoothed her waist and passed the brush over her own pompadour, looking critically at herself. "What is he like?"

"Nana, you'll never change. Of course I'll come with you, and we'll do the best we can."

I said it quickly, without thinking. What was it Father Flannery had told me? "You'll be all right wherever you go; you have your pack on your back." And I felt the answer to my life just then was that. It was the answer so long as I did not deny truth, nor faith in living, nor love.

She was still looking at herself, her head tilted to one side, the smile of Trojan Helen on her mouth, when the maid came in.

"There's visitors, miss, and Father Flannery to see you, and would you please to step downstairs?"

Nana helped me with my dress, and we left the room. We left my room, and my childhood and girlhood, we went down the stairs hand in hand, to take up my woman's life.

THIS BOOK IS SET IN GRANJON,

a type named in compliment to ROBERT GRANJON, type-cutter and printer—Antwerp, Lyons, Rome, Paris—active from 1523 to 1590. The boldest and most original designer of his time, he was one of the first to practise the trade of type-founder apart from that of printer.

This type face was designed by GEORGE W. JONES, who based his drawings upon a type used by CLAUDE GARAMOND (1510–61) in his beautiful French books, and more closely resembles Garamond's own than do any of the various modern types that bear his name.